THE EPISTLES
OF JOHN

THE EPISTLES
OF JOHN

by

DONALD W. BURDICK

MOODY PRESS

CHICAGO

Printed in the United States of America

CONTENTS

PREFACE

BEFORE A PERSON can properly use Scripture for his own spiritual development or for preaching or teaching, he must first discover the correct interpretation of the passage under consideration. Because of this priority and because of limited space, the primary concern of this brief commentary is interpretation. It therefore asks two basic questions of every passage:

       1. What does the passage say?
       2. What does it mean?

When these queries have been answered, the Bible student is ready to proceed to devotional or expository application.

The text employed is the King James (Authorized) Version. However, constant reference is made to the Greek text so the reader may have the full benefit of added light provided by the original language.

The analytical outlines of the epistles which appear in the introductions are also woven into the text of the commentary in order to enable the reader to follow the development of the thought of the books more readily. The commentary is thus a connected unity rather than a series of separate comments on isolated verses. The reader should keep his Bible before him when using the commentary. In addition, it is best to read the comments on an entire section rather than to limit oneself to remarks on the single verse being studied.

Progress from one verse to the next is indicated by verse numbers placed in parentheses within the text of the commentary. The purpose of this arrangement is to emphasize the unity of each epistle rather than introducing unnatural divisions which interrupt the progress of thought.

It is the author's sincere prayer that those who use this small volume will experience the illuminating assistance of the divine Teacher, the Holy Spirit, and that genuine growth in grace and spiritual knowledge will result from the study of this portion of God's Word.

1 JOHN

INTRODUCING THE EPISTLE

PROBABLY THE MOST DANGEROUS HERESY threatening the church of the first three centuries was Gnosticism. This deceptive teaching was built on the erroneous philosophical premise that all material substance is evil and that the nonmaterial, the spirit, is good. Man was considered fallen and lost because of being imprisoned in a material body. His only hope of salvation, according to the Gnostic, was through self-knowledge. (The term *Gnostic* is derived from the Greek word *gnōsis*, "knowledge.") Man is saved, not by faith, but by coming to know (1) his origin—a divine spark come from God—(2) his present condition—one of ignorance and imprisonment in evil matter—and (3) his potential destiny—a return to his original spiritual state.

Since matter was viewed as evil, the Gnostic became either an ascetic who sought to conquer the sinful desires of the flesh or a libertine who engaged in unbridled indulgence of the flesh. In this latter connection, some taught that matter or flesh could not affect the spirit; therefore one could engage in whatever acts he desired without ill effects upon his real self—his spirit.

Moreover, because the material body was thought to be sinful, it is obvious that God could not dwell in such a body. Consequently, the Gnostic could not believe in the incarnation of the Son of God. Some therefore held that Christ only appeared to possess a physical body. These have come to be designated docetists. Others said that the divine Christ came upon the human Jesus at His baptism (Mt 3:16) and left Him immediately before His death (Mt 27:46).

11

Gnosticism during the latter part of the first century had not yet reached its full development. Nevertheless, although it was as yet only in the incipient stages, the basic principles of the heresy were present.

According to early church writers, the father of the Gnostic heresy was Simon Magus who is referred to in Acts 8:9-13. Another Gnostic teacher was the Egyptian Jew named Cerinthus who taught that the divine Christ rested upon the human Jesus from baptism to crucifixion. It is also quite probable that the Nicolaitans whom John mentions in Revelation 2:6, 15 were Gnostics.

Such false teachers became a growing threat to the churches, with the assurance of some believers being shaken, and others actually defecting from the faith under Gnostic influence. One of the major areas affected was the province of Asia. For centuries Asia Minor had been a bridge across which a variety of religious and philosophical ideas flowed both from East to West and from West to East. The churches of Asia, in such cities as Ephesus, Smyrna, Pergamum, Thyatira, Sardis, Philadelphia and Laodicea (Rev 2-3), found themselves constantly pressured by heretical teachers of the Gnostic variety. It was to help the Asian believers resist the inroads of incipient Gnosticism that 1 John was written.

There is solid evidence both from early church Fathers and from the epistle itself that it was the apostle John who wrote this lovely but hard-hitting refutation of early Gnosticism. Without exception the Fathers who assign an author to the epistle, including Irenaeus, Clement of Alexandria, and Tertullian, declare him to have been John the apostle.

Internal evidence, as well, points to the same source. Such things as the simple Greek style, the eyewitness testimony, the authoritative manner, and the marks of intimacy, combine effectively to confirm the claims of the church Fathers.

It has been customary for liberal critics to reject apostolic authorship and to trace the epistle to some such person as an unknown disciple of John or another John called "the elder."

The latest scholarship, however, reveals a new attitude toward the historical trustworthiness of the Johannine writings, which, although it falls short of accepting apostolic authorship, nevertheless does provide added support for the traditional position.

Apparently about the time of the destruction of Jerusalem (A.D. 70) John left his homeland and came to spend the rest of his life in Ephesus. For the next quarter of a century the Asian churches were the objects of his special concern. Although many of the members had become Christians before he came to Asia, the aged apostle moved among the believers as a father among his children.

When the pressure of Gnosticism on the churches became too heavy, John wrote to his beloved children in the faith to warn them against the heresy and to confirm their assurance of salvation. Irenaeus (A.D. 140-203), who composed a major volume against the various Gnostic schools, informs us that John wrote to remove the error taught by Cerinthus and the Nicolaitans.[1]

There is reason to believe that 1 John was penned sometime after the fourth gospel. We may therefore date it between A.D. 90 and 95.

The letter is not addressed to the Gnostics with the purpose of disproving their error but, instead, is written to believers (2:12-14). It is basically a series of tests established to enable John's readers to distinguish between truth and error (4:6). Although they are stated in varying ways, there are two basic tests, the Christological and the ethical. The first requires acceptance of the fact that the Son of God came in human flesh as the incarnate God-Man (4:2-3). The second test is variously characterized as walking in the light, keeping God's commandments, doing righteousness, and loving the brothers. Thus, the essence of John's message is that he who is born of God (1) accepts the incarnation and (2) lives a life of righteousness and of love toward fellow believers.

These two standards serve both a negative and a positive purpose. Negatively, failure to measure up reveals that a person is not one of God's children. Positively, meeting the requirements provides a solid basis for the assurance of one's salvation (5:13).

John's theology is distinctively a theology of regeneration, just as Paul's is characteristically a theology of justification. To John salvation is a new birth into a new family, the family of God, the result of which is eternal life. One who is a member of this family will bear the family likeness of righteousness and of love. Because God is righteous, His offspring will practice righteousness (3:9); because God is love, His children will love one another (5:1).

The structure of 1 John is not easily discernible. At first glance, one may think that it really has no logical organization. Careful study, however, shows that the epistle is a very closely knit fabric of truth, difficult to unravel, but not without logical order. It is most intricately organized, similar in many ways to a symphonic composition. The student will discover several recurring themes—righteousness, love, and belief in the incarnation—around which interesting variations are developed, with each added treatment rising to a new height. The whole work comes to a grand finale (5:13-21) in which the keynote of the piece is sounded repeatedly with spine-tingling force. Over and over again John declares the fact of Christian assurance: We know that we have eternal life! We know that God answers prayer! We know that the Son of God has come!

It has become common to describe the organization of the epistle as a spiral. The accompanying figure is an adaptation of Lenski's diagram.[2] The introduction sounds the keynote of the incarnation of Christ. This is followed by three cycles of thought, each of which advances above and beyond the preceding section. In each cycle the discussion revolves around two recurring themes: (1) the correct view of Christ and (2) the resultant life of righteousness and love. The high point is reached in the concluding section where the grand theme of Christian assurance is heard again and again.

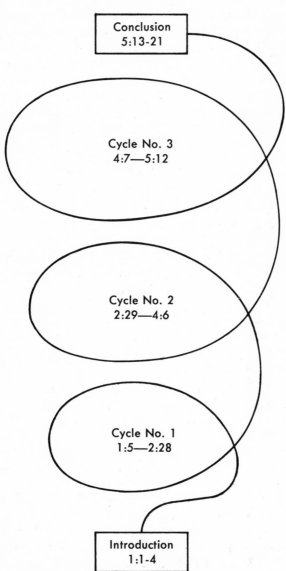

SPIRAL ORGANIZATION OF 1 JOHN

Conclusion
5:13-21

Cycle No. 3
4:7—5:12

Cycle No. 2
2:29—4:6

Cycle No. 1
1:5—2:28

Introduction
1:1-4

OUTLINE OF 1 JOHN

I. INTRODUCTION: THE REALITY OF THE INCARNATION (1:1-4)

   A. The Substance of the Apostolic Declaration (1:1-2)

   B. The Purpose of the Apostolic Declaration (1:3-4)

II. FIRST CYCLE: THE CHRISTIAN LIFE VIEWED AS FELLOWSHIP WITH THE FATHER AND THE SON (1:5—2:28)

   A. Fellowship Tested on Ethical Grounds (1:5—2:11)

      1. Fellowship demands moral likeness (1:5-7)

      2. Fellowship demands confession of sin (1:8—2:2)

      3. Fellowship demands obedience (2:3-6)

      4. Fellowship demands love of fellow believers (2:7-11)

   B. Two digressions (2:12-17)

      1. An assumption concerning the readers (2:12-14)

      2. A warning concerning loving the world (2:15-17)

   C. Fellowship Tested on Christological Grounds (2:18-28)

      1. The contrast between heretics and believers (2:18-21)

      2. The Christological test (2:22-23)

      3. The secret of continuing fellowship (2:24-28)

III. SECOND CYCLE: THE CHRISTIAN LIFE VIEWED AS DIVINE SONSHIP (2:29—4:6)

   A. Sonship Tested on Ethical Grounds (2:29—3:24)

      1. Sonship demands the practice of righteousness (2:29—3:10a)

COMMENTARY ON 1 JOHN

Introduction: The Reality of the Incarnation
(1:1-4)

VERSES 1-4 of chapter 1 comprise a striking introduction which sets the tone for the whole book. The Gnostic heresy attacked the person of Christ, the very heart of the Christian faith, so John opens his epistle with a ringing affirmation of the fact of the incarnation which the apostles had been declaring. The substance of that declaration appears in verses 1-2 and the purpose of it in verses 3-4. Understanding of this section will be facilitated by noting that verse 2 is a parenthesis and that verse 3 completes the statement begun in verse 1.

THE SUBSTANCE OF THE APOSTOLIC DECLARATION (1:1-2)

The fact which the apostles were declaring is set forth in five significant phrases (v. 1). John does not say that they were declaring *Him* who was from the beginning, but *"that which was from the beginning."* This neuter relative pronoun is to be related directly to the phrase "of the Word of life," which is better translated "concerning the Word of life." It was that which concerned the Word, Jesus Christ, that the apostles were proclaiming.

He is described first as existing from the beginning. When compared with John 1:1, the term "beginning" seems to refer to eternity past when the Word was with God the Father. This One who existed from eternity became incarnate and, John says, "We have heard" and "We have seen" Him. The Greek

18

perfect tense indicates that they heard and saw Him in the past and that the results were still present with them at the time of writing. What they heard is still ringing in their ears, and what they saw still lingers in their minds' eyes. It is clear that John is referring to seeing Jesus in the flesh for he says that they saw Him with their eyes.

In seeming repetition the apostle speaks of that "which we have looked upon." The Greek word used here *(theaomai)* describes a careful and deliberate inspection of the object in view. This kind of examination left no doubt in the apostles' minds that Jesus Christ possessed a real physical body. He was no phantom as some Gnostics taught. This is further confirmed by the factual statement that their hands actually handled Him, which would have been impossible had Jesus only seemed to have a human body. Some have suggested that John has particular reference to the postresurrection period (Lk 24:39; Jn 20:27).

The term "Word" *(logos)* used in reference to Christ occurs first in John 1:1, 14. Essentially it is an expression of revelation and communication. The spoken or written word reveals and communicates the mind of the speaker. The Word who was in essence Deity (Jn 1:1) took on human flesh (Jn 1:14). Prior to that event no one had ever seen God, but in the incarnation the Word revealed Him to men (Jn 1:18).

In 1 John 1:1 He is designated "the Word of life." He is not only the living Word, the source of life, but He is life itself, as verse 2 declares. It is thus best to understand the term "life" as being in apposition to the term "Word"—concerning the Word who is the life (Jn 1:4; 11:25; 14:6).

Before going on to complete his sentence—verse 1 contains only the direct object—John interrupts with the parenthetical statement of verse 2. His purpose is to explain more fully the incarnation which they had witnessed. For some thirty years, from birth to crucifixion, "the life was manifested"; and the apostles had seen it, not as a result of human discovery, but of divine revelation. It is obvious from the latter part of the

verse that the life is personal, for He was "with the Father."
The Greek preposition *pros* speaks of active, face-to-face, personal communion (cf. Jn 1:1, "the Word was *with* God") .

Instead of designating Him as "the Word of life" as he does
in verse 1, John in verse 2 uses the more direct designation
"the life." In Himself, essentially, the Son of God *is* the life.
And He is further characterized as "that eternal life." The
word *aiōnios* may be used of a long but limited period of time,
but in the New Testament it almost always refers to that which,
like God, is eternal (Ro 16:26; 2 Co 4:18; Heb 9:14) . The
expression "eternal life" is both quantitative and qualitative,
referring to the length of the life as well as the kind of life.
It is unending life, but it is also life which is characterized by
such qualities as spirituality, glory, abundance, holiness and
love. In Christ this life, both quantitative and qualitative, is
personified. He *is* "that eternal life."

It was this life, personified and revealed in Christ, which the
apostles had seen and still remembered (Greek perfect tense) .
Now they are bearing witness to what they had seen, not a
momentary testimony, but a continuing declaration (Greek
present tense) , which for John had spanned some sixty years.
Not only was this declaration a personal testimony, but it also
had the character of an official and authoritative proclamation
(*apaggellomen,* "show") . The apostles were officially com-
missioned by Christ and sent forth with His authority to preach
the gospel (Mt 28:18-20) .

THE PURPOSE OF THE APOSTOLIC DECLARATION (1:3-4)

Having completed his parenthetical explanation (v. 2) ,
John resumes the sentence begun in verse 1. In order to tie the
direct-object clauses of verse 1 to the remainder of the sentence (v. 3) , he repeats a portion of verse 1—"That which we
have seen and heard." Likewise he repeats the verb *apaggellomen* from verse 2. There it is translated "shew"; here, "declare."

The apostolic purpose in making this continuing declaration of the incarnation was that their hearers might "have fellowship" with the apostles. The present tense verb "may have" indicates that John has no momentary relationship in mind. It is to be a continuing experience. *Koinōnia* ("fellowship") is related to *koinos* ("common"), which was used in secular Greek to refer to things held in common. Fellowship, then, is based on something held in common by two or more persons. The context makes it clear that what is here to be held in common is the truth of the incarnation of God's Son. Without acceptance of this fundamental doctrine of the Christian faith there can be no such thing as fellowship in the New Testament sense of the word.

John emphasizes the fact that this fellowship is not merely a human relationship. The full force of his statement could be represented as follows: "And certainly the fellowship of which I have spoken, that which is ours, is with the Father, and with his Son, Jesus Christ." To place one's faith in the incarnate Christ is to enter a fellowship which includes God the Father and God the Son as well as all those who possess saving faith.

It is noteworthy that John's use of the term *koinōnia* does not justify its limitation to the small group of the spiritual elite. The breadth of its usage is to be seen in the fact that New Testament *koinōnia* is first of all fellowship with God. To be a Christian is the same as being in fellowship with Him. Christ made this clear when He said, "And this is life eternal, that they might *know* thee the only true God and Jesus Christ, whom thou hast sent " (Jn 17:3). Thus, the New Testament *koinōnia* includes all who are saved.

Viewed vertically, fellowship with God demands likeness to God in moral goodness (1 Jn 1:5-7). On the horizontal plane, fellowship with other believers involves love toward all the members of the family of God (1 Jn 5:1). *Koinōnia* is not merely a gathering where confessions of weakness and sin are shared. It is a mutual relationship which includes God and all of His people. The cement which binds this true *koinōnia* together is a love that is not mere sentiment, but which expresses itself by gladly sharing financially and materially with one's fellows who are in need.

The declaration which is spoken of in verses 2-3 is the broader proclamation which the apostles had been carrying everywhere since the resurrection of Christ. In verse 4 John limits his statement of purpose to the epistle which he is writing. The same message which the apostles had been proclaiming generally (vv. 1-3), John as the representative of the apostolic group now writes to the churches of Asia—"These things write we unto you."

The purpose of this epistle is "that your joy may be full." The earliest Greek manuscripts read "our joy," which, on careful examination, makes good sense. If his readers profit by what he writes, the author will have reason to rejoice. The verbal form "may be full" is particularly significant, referring as it does to the continuing results of a past action. John writes so that joy may come to the point of fullness and remain in the state of being full. This is a forceful way of speaking of a continuing state of joy.

First Cycle: The Christian Life Viewed as Fellowship with the Father and the Son (1:5—2:28)

In the introduction (1:1-4) John has laid the foundation for his epistle upon the bedrock fact of the incarnation. Those who in faith receive this truth enter a unique fellowship with all those who possess like precious faith, but, what is more important, they enter a life of fellowship with the Father and with His Son. It is this fact which provides the keynote for the first major section of the epistle (1:5—2:28). The Christian life is a life of fellowship with God. Therefore, not to be in a fellowship relationship is not to be a Christian.

In this first cycle of John's argument the claim to enjoy

saving fellowship with God is submitted to two basic tests: the ethical (1:5—2:11) and the Christological (2:18-28).

FELLOWSHIP TESTED ON ETHICAL GROUNDS (1:5—2:11)

The ethical test of fellowship is concerned with such matters as walking in the light (1:5-7), confession of sin (1:8—2:2), obedience to God's commands (2:3-6) and love for fellow believers (2:7-11).

FELLOWSHIP DEMANDS MORAL LIKENESS (1:5-7)

The standard (1:5). John opens this section with a declaration of the standard by which fellowship is to be tested. It is none other than the character of God Himself. This truth is one which the apostles had heard from Christ during His earthly ministry.

It is obvious that the term "light" is used metaphorically. God's nature is described as possessing characteristics which may be illustrated by light. Although John does not explicitly state what aspects of light he has in mind, we may find some indication in the immediate context and in his usage of the term elsewhere. In verse 6 he speaks of practicing the truth, and in verses 8-10 he refers to the confession of sin. In John 3:19-21, where John is also discussing "the light," practicing the truth is the opposite of practicing evil. It would seem, therefore, that John employs the term "light" to represent moral goodness—truth, righteousness and holiness. And this, he declares, is what God in His essence is.

Having made a positive assertion—"God is light"—he backs it up with a negative statement—"In him is no darkness at all." If light is a figure for moral goodness, darkness must represent moral evil. In God there is no moral imperfection, whether in nature, attitude or action. This detail is stressed by the employment of a Greek double negative, which is always emphatic. Furthermore, the word translated "at all" is a compound word literally meaning "not one." John, therefore, says, "In God there is no darkness, not even one bit."

After establishing the standard for testing in verse 5, John then proceeds to set forth the test, negatively stated in verse 6 and positively stated in verse 7.

The negative result (1:6). This verse contains three elements: (1) the claim—"If we say that we have fellowship with him"; (2) the test—"and walk in darkness"; (3) the result of the test—"we lie, and do not the truth."

The claim is a profession of continuing fellowship with God, as the present tense verb "have" indicates. This is the same as claiming to be in a saving relationship with God; it is professing to know Him personally.

The question which John in reality raises is this: Does the claimant really possess saving knowledge of God? In order to answer this question, the person's walk is examined. The term "walk" is a figure of speech referring to the conduct of one's life. Since God is light (v. 5) and fellowship is the experience of having something in common (see comment on v. 3), the person who is in fellowship with God must share the characteristics of God. He must be walking in the light. If, however, he is found to be walking habitually (Greek present tense) in darkness, there is no basis for his claim to fellowship. Since darkness represents moral evil (see comment on v. 5), walking in darkness is a figurative expression for living a life of sin. One who lives such a life cannot have fellowship with God who is holy, because the two have nothing in common on which their fellowship can be based.

The result of the test, therefore, is that the claimant is shown to be lying and not practicing the truth. The present tense "do" speaks of continued practice. It is noteworthy that truth is not something merely to be believed; it is to be practiced in daily life.

The positive result (1:7). The claim to have fellowship with God, which in verse 6 is explicitly stated, is here assumed. John moves directly to a statement of (1) the test—"if we walk in the light, as he is in the light," and (2) the result of the test—

"we have fellowship one with another, and the blood of Jesus Christ his Son cleanseth us from all sin."

Here again the test is an examination of the claimant's conduct to see if it supports his profession of fellowship. Just as walking in darkness represented living a life of sin, so walking in the light depicts a life of moral goodness. John does not have in mind any temporary expression of righteousness, for he uses the present tense of the verb "walk," which speaks of linear action, a continuing habit of life. We are reminded again of the standard established in verse 5. The believer is to walk in the light as God "is in the light."

If we live lives characterized by moral goodness we have something in common with God. Moral likeness is evident. The test has shown a positive result. It proves that we are having continued fellowship (Greek present tense) with God. Here, however, John broadens the circle of fellowship. The expression "one with another" (v. 7) suggests relationship between more or less equal parties, and thus fellowship between believers must be in view. But such fellowship is, in turn, the sign of divine fellowship. As verse 3 indicates, the two are inseparably bound together.

The second fact which the test shows to be true is that the claimant is being cleansed from sin by Christ's blood. This is not a statement of a past, once-for-all cleansing. Instead, the present tense "cleanseth" describes an action in progress at the present time. The person who is walking in the light normally lives a life of righteousness, but when he does slip and sin (2:1) he makes it a practice to confess his sin and to receive present cleansing from God.

In summary, like the false teachers against whom John writes, we may claim to have a saving knowledge of God; but if our lives show no moral likeness to God, our claim is false. If, on the other hand, our lives are marked by holiness, we in this way confirm our claim to be in saving relationship to Him.

FELLOWSHIP DEMANDS CONFESSION OF SIN (1:8—2:2)

Since God is light, no one can enter into fellowship with Him unless he is willing to confess his sin. After applying this test of confession with negative results in 1:8, 10 and with positive results in 1:9, John briefly states the theological underpinnings of confession (2:1-2).

The test of confession applied (1:8-10). John's readers were confronted with false teachers who not only lived in sin but who denied moral responsibility. Their claim "We have no sin" was a denial that they possessed any indwelling depravity. It is this profession that John proceeds to examine (v. 8). The test, although assumed, is not explicitly stated, probably because the apostle takes it for granted that his readers know the clear Scripture teaching that no one is without sin (Ps 14:1-3). When this high-sounding claim to be sinless is viewed in the light of the biblical principle, it is seen to be obviously false. If we profess to be without sin we show that we are self-deceived and ignorant of God's revealed truth. In order for a person to be saved he must first of all admit that he is a sinner. Therefore, one who refuses to make such an admission cannot possibly be in fellowship with God.

On the other hand, "if we confess our sins" we will find forgiveness and cleansing (v. 9). This is the positive statement which John places in contrast to verse 8. Instead of denial, there is open verbal admission of sins (cf. Mt 3:6). The forgiveness and cleansing which follow are necessary for a person to be in fellowship with God. It must be remembered that this epistle was written to those who already are forgiven (2:12). John is not here speaking of the initial forgiveness of sin which occurs at the point of salvation. At that time the guilt of all one's sins—past, present and future—is forgiven. The forgiveness of this verse, however, is an experience which comes after salvation. Its function is to remove that which has disturbed the believer's fellowship with God. Whereas the former is a legal remission of guilt, the latter is the Father's forgiveness of His child to restore undisturbed communion.

To those who confess their sins, this forgiveness, like initial forgiveness, is assured by the faithfulness and justice of God. He is loyal to His promise (Jer 31:34) and bound by His righteousness to forgive all who repent and confess.

In verse 10 the epistle returns to the negative aspect of the test of confession. Here, however, the claim is not that "we have *no sin*" but that "we have *not sinned.*" Whereas verse 8 contains the denial of sin as an indwelling principle of depravity, verse 10 refers to the denial of acts of sin. Both claims are contrary to God's Word. Therefore, if we make such assertions, we are making God out to be a liar because we deny the truth of His Word. Hence it is clear that His Word does not dwell in our hearts. Such things cannot be true of a person who is in a saving relationship with God.

The theological foundations of confession (2:1-2). These verses point out two foundation stones upon which the practice of confession rests: Christ's intercessory work (2:1) and Christ's propitiatory work (2:2).

John introduces these remarks with a term of endearment "my little children," which is in keeping with his emphasis on the new birth and the family of God. The Greek word *teknia* literally means "little born ones."

One of the apostle's purposes in writing these dear ones was that they might not commit even one act of sin, as the tense of the verb indicates. However, recognizing that our sanctification is not yet complete, God has made provision for those occasions when believers do commit acts of sin. Walking in the light does not demand sinless perfection. This verse, on the other hand, does not condone the continual practice of sin, for John actually writes, "If any man commits sin" (Greek aorist tense), not "If any man is practicing sin" (Greek present tense). Walking in the light, of necessity, includes confession of those acts of sin which the believer commits. And forgiveness is guaranteed, for "we have an advocate with the Father."

In Greek legal usage an advocate (*paraklētos*) was usually a friend of the defendant called to testify concerning the character of the latter or to intercede for him. And this is what Jesus does for us. He appears, as it were, in heaven's court and intercedes for us when we sin. The same term (*paraklētos*) is used by our Lord to explain the relationship of the Holy Spirit to the believer in His ministry as Comforter, Intercessor or Helper (Jn 14:16, 26; 15:26; 16:7).

The second basis for the practice of confession is the fact that "he is the propitiation for our sins" (v. 2). The same One who now intercedes for us first of all offered Himself as a propitiation to avert the just wrath of God against sin. This is no arbitrary anger on God's part. Our sin deserved His wrath, but Christ provided satisfaction for divine justice. This propitiatory act was not merely sufficient for the sins of those who believe; it was an adequate atonement for "the sins of the whole world." Apart from this gracious work of the Saviour, there can be no forgiveness of sins; but because He died and now intercedes for us, forgiveness is available to those who confess their wrongdoings.

FELLOWSHIP DEMANDS OBEDIENCE (2:3-6)

This section (2:3-6) is a repetition of the test found in 1:5-7, using different terms and figures of speech and introducing the additional idea of love for fellow believers. After giving a general statement of the test of obedience (2:3), John applies the test first with negative and then positive results (2:4-5). The passage concludes with a summary statement (2:6).

General statement of the test (2:3). Instead of using the term *fellowship* to describe the believer's relation to God, John now speaks of knowing Christ. The two concepts are parallel: to have fellowship with a person is to know him, and vice versa. Furthermore, to "walk in the light" (1:7) is to "keep his commandments" (2:3). The context (2:1-2, 6) indicates that the pronouns "him" and "his" refer to Christ rather than to God the Father.

The knowledge of which John writes is neither theoretical nor speculative, as was claimed by the Gnostic heretics; it is experiential and personal. Notice that the passage does not speak of knowing *about* Him, but of knowing *Him*. This kind of knowledge can only come from the experience of personal contact with Him. To know Christ in this way is to enjoy a saving relationship to Him.

The assurance that this relationship is a reality is here based not on feeling or mere profession of faith but on the observable evidence of continuing obedience to His commandments. The present tense "keep" reveals that John is not speaking of temporary or spasmodic obedience but of habitual practice. Although the commandments are limited in 3:22-24 to belief in Christ and love for others, the context immediately preceding 2:3 seems to point to a more general usage here, including the divine commands in general. Such a test ruled out the validity of the Gnostic claim to spiritual knowledge, for the antinomian teachers against whom 1 John was written knew nothing of obedience to Christ's commands.

Application of the test (2:4-5). Continuing his pattern of contrast, the author states the test of obedience with negative results (v. 4) and then with positive results (v. 5). The first statement contains (1) the claim—"He that saith, I know him" (2) the test—"keepeth not his commandments," and (3) the result of the test—"is a liar, and the truth is not in him." Profession of faith is here declared to be insufficient in itself. Knowledge which is not accompanied by obedience fails the test and is proved to be counterfeit. John does not say that such a person is merely deceived, but that he himself is a deceiver ("liar"). Like the one who refuses to admit that he is a sinner (1:8), he does not possess the truth, especially that understanding of spiritual things which realizes that genuine knowledge of Christ must be accompanied by a life of obedience.

In stating the positive results of the test of obedience John does not repeat the claim since it is the same as in verse 4. Thus in verse 5 he only includes (1) the test—"whoso keepeth his word," and (2) the results—"in him verily is the love of God perfected: hereby [by this] know we that we are in him." Here again the verb "keepeth," being in the present tense, depicts continuing action. The person who passes the test of obedience does so by being habitually obedient. For the sake of variety, John here refers to the commandments as "his word."

Habitual obedience on the part of a person who claims to know Christ demonstrates two facts. First, love for God is perfected in him. That the apostle means love *for* God rather than love of which God is the source is suggested by the relationship of love and obedience. Love naturally results in doing the will of the one loved. In John 14:21 Jesus said, "He that hath my commandments, and keepeth them, he it is that loveth me." Since no one reaches perfection in this life, it is better to view the perfection of love as referring to love which reaches its goal of producing obedience. Love which does not result in action is incomplete, but love which moves us to do the Lord's will finds its proper fulfillment in action.

The second fact demonstrated by obedience is that "we are in him." In view of the terms used in verses 3-4, we would expect John to say that obedience proves that we "know him." It seems best, therefore, to understand the words "we are in him" as synonymous with the expression "we know him" (v. 3). By varying his terminology the apostle explains more fully what he means by knowing Christ. To know Him is to be in an intimate, mystical relationship with Him. This is not a casual acquaintance; it is a relationship of intimate fellowship (cf. 1:6-7). The only sure indication of such an association is obedience which springs from love.

Summary statement (2:6). In this recapitulation John draws a lesson from the test of obedience. We "ought . . . to walk . . . as he walked." In 1:5—2:28 the Christian life is viewed as being one of fellowship with God. To be saved is to be in fellowship with Him. This concept of fellowship has previously been expressed as knowing Christ (2:3-4) and as being in Him

(2:5). Now John refers to the experience as abiding "in him." The word "abide" (*menō*) speaks of a continuing and intimate relationship rather than a temporary, superficial association. The idea of continuing action inherent in the meaning of the verb is strengthened by the use of the present tense. This concept of abiding no doubt comes from John 15 where Jesus declares that the fruit-bearing branch is the one which stands in a continuing vital relationship to the vine.

The one who claims such a relationship is under an ever present obligation "to walk, even as he walked." As in 1:6-7, the term "walk" is a figure of speech depicting the conduct of one's life. That the pronoun "he" refers to Christ is indicated by the statement that "he walked," which could not be said of God the Father. Thus, John is declaring that we are to live habitually (Greek present tense) just as Christ lived. This comparison is parallel to that of walking "in the light, as he is in the light" (1:7). Just as the ideas of fellowship—knowing Him, being in Him and abiding in Him—are parallel, so the concepts of walking in the light, keeping His commandments, and walking as He walked are synonymous.

FELLOWSHIP DEMANDS LOVE OF FELLOW BELIEVERS (2:7-11)

The section 2:7-11 begins in a striking manner employing paradox to point up the test of love. First, the command to love is described as being both old and new (2:7-8). Then, the test of love is applied, twice with negative results (2:9, 11) and once with positive results (2:10).

Some commentators in outlining 1 John distinguish between the ethical test of fellowship (1:5—2:6) and the test based on love (2:7-11).[3] There is good reason, however, to view the two as one and the same test. Jesus spoke of the intimate relation between love and the law (Mt 22:37-40), and Paul declared love to be the fulfilling of the law (Ro 13:8-10). To love, therefore, is the same as keeping Christ's commandments (1 Jn 2:3-6). It is in reality an ethical obligation.

The commandment described (2:7-8). The better Greek
manuscripts begin this verse with the word *beloved* rather than
"brethren." It is significant that the initial occurrence of
agapētoi ("beloved") in 1 John is here in 2:7 where the theme
of love is first introduced. From the expression "new commandment" (v. 8) and the discussion of love in verses 9-11, we may
be sure that the command of verses 7-8 is the command to love.
John declares that the commandment he has in mind is not a
novel or strange kind of commandment. His readers had long
been familiar with it, having had it "from the beginning." The
time indicated by the term "beginning" cannot be the same
here as in 1:1. There it describes eternity past; here it speaks
of the beginning of the readers' Christian experience. John is
reminding them of an old, familiar commandment of long
standing. The verb "had," being the Greek imperfect tense,
lays stress on their constant possession of the command through
the years.

It is apparent that the specific statement which the apostle
had in mind is the declaration of Jesus, "A new commandment
I give unto you, That ye love one another; as I have loved you,
that ye also love one another" (Jn 13:34). "The word" which
they had "heard from the beginning" was the apostolic message
containing this injunction to love their brothers in Christ.

In spite of his denial that he is speaking of a new commandment, in verse 8 the apostle explicitly declares, "A new commandment I write unto you." This obviously is paradox.
When the commandment is examined from one point of view,
it is not new, for John's readers had possessed it since their conversion. However, when it is seen from another point of view
it *is* new.

There are two spheres in which this old command is new.
First, the newness "is true in him," that is, in Christ. His self-
giving death gave new meaning to the old law of love (Lev
19:18). In Him the world witnessed a new demonstration of
what love really is. And He, in turn, commanded His disciples
to love one another as He had loved them (Jn 13:34).

The second sphere in which the old command is new is "in you." It is new in the believer's experience, as John points out in the explanatory clause, "because the darkness is past, and the true light now shineth." The verb "is past" is the translation of the Greek present tense *paragetai* which literally means "is passing away." It is not that the darkness is completely gone, which would be contrary to our experience, but the darkness is declared to be in the process of now passing away. In its place as it is receding, the true light is already shining. This is true in the lives of individual believers as they grow in grace. Thus, the newness of the command to love one another is a newness of daily experience as the believer grows in love and increasingly overcomes sin and hatred.

The test of love applied (2:9-11). Verse 9 falls into three sections: (1) the claim—"He that saith he is in the light," (2) the test—"and hateth his brother," and (3) the result—"is in darkness even until now." To be in the light is practically synonymous with walking in the light, for both refer to a life lived in the sphere of truth and holiness. No doubt the Gnostics also claimed to be in the light, but to them it merely meant the possession of esoteric knowledge. It was therefore necessary that their claim be tested to see if it was genuine.

For this purpose John employs the test of love, not love for the world at large, but love for one's brother in Christ. First John is the family epistle in which God is seen as the Father and believers as brothers in the family. This relationship is most clearly set forth in 5:1. John is speaking of love for one who is a brother by regeneration as well as by creation.

If a person habitually hates God's people (Greek present tense), this is an indication that he is "in darkness," which for John is to be separated from God who is light (1:5). And the one who hates his fellow Christian is in darkness "even until now." This is the same as saying that he has always been in darkness and has never entered the light. Such a person cannot claim to be in fellowship with God (1:6).

The claim in verse 10 to be in the light is to be assumed as continuing from verse 9. Thus John moves directly to the test—"He that loveth his brother," and then to the results of the test—"abideth in the light, and there is none occasion of stumbling in him." This application of the test finds that the person being tested "loveth his brother." The use of the present tense indicates that this is not a momentary flash of affection; instead it is a continuing attitude toward one's fellow Christian. John does not necessarily refer to constant, perfect love any more than walking in the light (1:7) demands perfection in holiness, as is indicated by the provision made for confession (1:9). Although the general attitude toward other believers is one of love, there may be occasions when the Christian allows other attitudes to creep in.

The habitual practice of loving fellow believers is proof that the one loving "abideth in the light." His claim to dwell in the light is confirmed by his relationships with his associates in the faith, and this, in turn, demonstrates that he is in fellowship with God. Assurance in this case is based not upon feeling or mere profession but upon love for the people of God.

In the second place the test shows that "there is none occasion of stumbling" in the person being tested. The word *skandalon*, translated "occasion of stumbling," was used to refer (1) to a bait stick on a trap or (2) to a stumbling block. In this context, it seems best to understand John as saying that there is no stumbling block in the pathway of the one who is loving his brother. Since he is not in darkness he can see where he is going (cf. v. 11).

Apparently for the purpose of emphasis verse 11 restates the test of love from the negative point of view. The one whose habitual attitude toward his fellow believer is that of hatred is really not one of God's redeemed. He is yet in the darkness of sin and error as John previously declared in verse 9. Now, the apostle adds force to his declaration by piling up additional statements, one on the other: (1) he "walketh in darkness," (2) he "knoweth not whither he goeth," and (3) the "darkness hath blinded his eyes." Because the activity of his life is habitually carried on in the sphere of darkness, he can only wander on aimlessly with no sense of direction. The verb "goeth" literally means to depart. Thus the one who continually hates is not aware of what his destiny is nor of the way he is traveling. Blindly he moves on toward the "blackness of darkness" which will be forever (Jude 13).

TWO DIGRESSIONS (2:12-17)

The continuity of the closely woven argument of the epistle is broken at this point by two brief parenthetical sections, neither of which is altogether unrelated to the book's main thrust. The first digression states the author's assumption concerning the spiritual state of the readers (2:12-14), and the second sets forth a warning against loving the world (2:15-17).

AN ASSUMPTION CONCERNING THE READERS (2:12-14)

In the foregoing portion of the epistle John has bluntly denounced persons who claim to have fellowship with God but who walk in darkness (1:6), deny their own sinfulness (1:8, 10), do not obey Christ's commands (2:4), and hate their brothers in Christ (2:9, 11). Now, lest his readers misunderstand, the apostle interrupts the course of his discussion to assure them that these pointed statements are not directed against them. He wants them to understand that he is addressing them as believers who know Jesus Christ as Saviour. John's purpose in writing is not to shake the confidence of God's people but to give them more adequate ground for assurance.

The main feature of this section is repetition for the sake of emphasis. Six parallel statements, arranged in two series of three, are advanced one after the other. Each series of three is addressed consecutively to children, fathers and young men.

In verse 12 John addresses himself to "little children," a descriptive he first uses in 2:1. There it is a term of endearment obviously referring to all the recipients of the epistle. It would, therefore, seem reasonable to assume that all the readers are likewise included in the usage in verse 12. This is confirmed by the fact that the age groups are not listed in the natural order—children, young men, fathers.

The reason why John is concerned about these people is that their "sins are forgiven." Because they are children of God he feels it necessary to warn them against the Gnostic error which is threatening them. The forgiveness of which this verse speaks is the initial remission of the guilt of all sins—past, present and future. This forgiveness is to be distinguished from the Father's repeated forgiveness of His child each time he confesses his sin and seeks restoration of undisturbed communion (1 Jn 1:9). Both types of forgiveness are granted "for his name's sake." In Scripture the term *name* often is used to refer to the character of the person who bears the name (Ps 44:5; Ac 3:16; 3 Jn 7). Thus the believer's forgiveness rests upon the person and work of Christ. We are forgiven on account of His merit, not because of anything we may be or do.

Having addressed all of his readers as "little children" (v. 12), the apostle next directs his words to the "fathers" (v. 13). This term must be understood in a more limited sense as referring to believers who are older, whether physically or spiritually or both. Inasmuch as Paul had begun his ministry in Ephesus almost forty years previously, it is certain that there were Asian believers of long standing. These would have been men who were mature in the faith as well as leaders in the churches. It is altogether fitting, since knowledge comes with maturity, that John should characterize them as knowing "him that is from the beginning." Comparison with 1:1 reveals that the One who is "from the beginning" can be no other than God the Son who became our incarnate Saviour. Notice that he does not say that they knew *about* Him but that they knew *Him*. Knowledge in the biblical sense is never speculative nor theoretical. Instead it is always related to experience, both growing out of experience and resulting in added experience. These older believers knew Him because they had met and personally experienced Him. Their knowledge was far superior to the esoteric or private knowledge claimed by those initiated into Gnosticism.

John next turns his attention to the "young men" *(neaniskoi)*. This word was commonly used to designate persons between the ages of twenty-four and forty. No doubt these were men who were younger both in physical and in spiritual age. It is in keeping with the characteristics of this age level that the writer addresses them as having "overcome the wicked one." This victory is, first, an accomplished fact which occurred when these young men turned from sin and error to faith in Christ (5:4-5), but it is also a continuing experience in the everyday battle of the life of faith.

The apostle now begins his second series of three parallel statements in his attempt to drum into his readers' minds the fact that he is sure of the genuineness of their salvation. Whereas in verse 12 he uses *teknia,* which literally means "little born ones," in verse 13 he employs *paidia,* a term which describes the "little children" as being subordinate to the authority of those who are older. As in verse 12, "little children" includes all believers (cf. v. 18 where *paidia* also occurs). In verse 12 the little children are characterized as being forgiven; here they are described as knowing the Father. Not only do they know Him as God, but as a Father who loves and cares for His own. This is the same as saying that they have eternal life (Jn 17:3).

On John's second address to fathers (v. 14), see comment on v. 13. The second statement about the young men is the same as the previous one, but it adds two explanatory clauses: (1) "Ye are strong" and (2) "the word of God abideth in you." Strength is the normal characteristic of youth. These young men were spiritually strong because the word of God was dwelling in them continually (Greek present tense). As a result they had overcome the devil.

A WARNING CONCERNING LOVING THE WORLD (2:15-17)

The second digression from the main argument of the epistle

deals with the Christian's attitude toward the world. In the section immediately preceding these two digressions John has discussed love for fellow Christians as a necessary mark of genuine salvation (2:7-11). There love for believers is commanded; here (2:15-17) love for the world is condemned.

The prohibition "Love not the world" (v. 15) is better translated "Stop loving the world," since the Greek verb is the present tense imperative used with the negative particle. The writer, as this construction shows, assumes that his readers do have some affection for the world. In this passage the term "world" does not refer to the world of people (Jn 3:16) nor to the created world (Jn 17:24), but to the evil world order controlled by Satan. It includes all that goes to make up the organized system of evil on this earth. God's people are to stop setting their esteem on the world as a thing of value, as the Greek word *agapate* ("love") indicates. "The things that are in the world" are not necessarily material items, although these may be involved. As verse 16 reveals, John has in mind men's attitudes toward things rather than the material things themselves.

Findlay has said, " 'The world' is not made up of so many outward objects that can be specified; it is the sum of those influences emanating from men and things around us, which draw us away from God."[4] John's readers are being warned against becoming so involved in the world that they are emotionally tied to it and come to value it as a way of life. Although Christians are of necessity in the world, they are not to be intimately related to the world. Its things, its ways, its attitudes, its spirit are not to be held dear by the people of God.

Verses 15b-17 set forth two reasons why Christians should not love the world: (1) the antagonism between God and the world (vv. 15b-16) and (2) the temporary nature of the world (v. 17). Love for God and love for the world are mutually exclusive. "If any man [habitually] love [Greek present tense] the world," he does not possess love for God (v. 15b). In terms reminiscent of Matthew 6:24, John here speaks of love as supreme devotion which excludes all other loyalties. A person can be totally devoted to God or to the world, but not to both at the same time.

Continuing his explanation of the antagonism existing between God and the evil world system, John next points out that none of the elements which make up this wicked system find their source in God, but in the world (v. 16). "The lust of the flesh" is the passionate desire for self-satisfaction which springs from the corrupt, sinful tendency resident in man's nature. The term "flesh" does not refer to the physical body; it speaks of the lower aspect of sinful human nature, that which is sensual. "The lust of the eyes," on the other hand, refers to the higher aspects of sinful human nature. It is the inordinate desire to "feast the eyes" on things which are seen, whether good or bad. "The pride of life" is that proud pretension which glories in material things. It is the attitude which assumes that one is more than he really is, simply because of his many material possessions; it is the spirit which is boastfully confident in wealth rather than in God, assuming that one's life consists of that which one possesses (Dan 4:30; Lk 12:16-21). Attitudes such as these, so characteristic of this evil world, are in diametric opposition to God. It is therefore imperative that God's people stop loving the world and, instead, direct the devotion of their hearts toward Him.

The second reason for not loving the world is that "the world passeth away" (v. 17). The present tense indicates that it is even now in the process of dissolution. By its very nature evil is self-destructive. The world system of evil carries within itself forces which are causing its own deterioration; and ultimately when Christ returns to establish His kingdom, He will completely destroy it.

In contrast to the transient world characterized by lust and proud pretension, John describes the one "that doeth the will of God." The present tense verb reveals that the apostle has in mind the continual practice of God's will. As we have seen before (2:3-6), obedience is the persistent characteristic of the one who possesses a saving knowledge of Christ. Whereas the evil world is passing away, God's child will continue forever in unending enjoyment of abundant life. The idea of permanency receives triple stress from the meaning of the verb "abideth," from the continuing action signified by the present tense, and from the Greek idiom *eis ton aiōna,* meaning "forever."

Fellowship Tested on Christological Grounds (2:18-28)

At this point the author turns his attention from the ethical (1:5—2:11) to the doctrinal (2:18-28) test of fellowship. The standard which he uses as a test is truth, particularly the truth which concerns the person of Christ (2:22-23). Only he who believes "that Jesus is the Christ" has fellowship with God. That John is continuing to view the Christian life as fellowship with God is evident from the references to continuing or abiding in the Father and in the Son (2:24, 27-28). The Gnostics, by their rejection of Jesus as the incarnate Christ, clearly demonstrated that they had never entered this saving relationship of fellowship. This section sets forth (1) the contrast between heretics and believers (2:18-21), (2) the Christological test (2:22-23), and (3) the secret of continuing fellowship (2:24-28).

THE CONTRAST BETWEEN HERETICS AND BELIEVERS (2:18-21)

The heretics (2:18-19). Repeating his term of endearment, "little children," the author tells his readers that they are in "the last time." Similar statements occur in Hebrews 1:2 and 1 Peter 1:20. The New Testament speaks of two ages, the present age and the age to come (Mk 10:30). According to Paul (Gal 1:4), the present age is characterized by evil and therefore must include the time from the fall of Adam to the second advent of Christ. It is to the latter portion of this period, from the cross to the second coming, that John and others refer by the use of the expressions "last hour," "last days" and "last times." During the millennia before the cross, God's program of redemption found its beginnings; at the cross redemption was accomplished; the time since the cross is the concluding portion of the age.

That this is the last hour is revealed by the presence of "many antichrists." Just as *the* Antichrist, the archenemy of the Lord and His people, will come during the days of the great tribulation, so now he is preceded by many who manifest in miniature his spirit of antagonism toward God. These are the false teachers who, according to Christ, are characteristic of this present age (Mt 24:11). John's specific reference was to the Gnostics of his day.

Apparently these false teachers had once moved in the circle of believers, professing to be genuine Christians, but then they "went out" (2:19), that is, they severed their relations with God's people. The same Greek preposition *(ek)* is used in each of the first two clauses of the verse. "They went out from [*ek*] us, but they were not of [*ek*] us." Apparently they removed themselves bodily from the fellowship of believers because spiritually they had nothing in common. As John makes clear in 1:1-4, fellowship is based on holding the truth of the incarnation in common. Those who possess like precious faith continue in fellowship with one another. Thus, if the Gnostics had been in harmony with the believers "they would . . . have continued" with them. The Authorized Version's italicized words "no doubt" are not based on the original text. John has made it clear that the perseverance of the saints is proof of their genuineness. Stott well says, "Endurance is the half-mark of the saved."[5]

Although the Authorized Version's italicized words "they went out" are not in the Greek text, it is evident that some such expression must be supplied. The departure of the false teachers from the Christian circle served a divine purpose, namely, to show that "they were not all of us." The Greek word order suggests that the departure revealed that none of those who left possessed a vital and genuine relationship to the community of the saved. The statement should be translated, "in order that they might be manifest that none of them were of us."

The believers (2:20-21). In contrast to the anti-Christian teachers who left the fellowship of the saved, John's readers "have an unction from the Holy One" (2:20). They have been anointed with an anointing which comes from God. This anointing does not come *from* the Holy Spirit; instead it *is* the Holy Spirit whom God the Father sends. In 2:27 the anointing is said to perform the function of teaching, an act possible only for a personal being.

According to the Authorized Version those who possess this anointing from the Holy One "know all things," which is a most pretentious claim. The better Greek text, however, reads, "and you all know." Believers do not possess all knowledge, but they all possess knowledge of spiritual truth. The Gnostics boasted that they alone enjoyed genuine knowledge. To counteract this false claim, John assured his readers that they, by virtue of the indwelling Holy Spirit, were the recipients of true spiritual knowledge. They were far more knowledgeable in spiritual things than were the Gnostic boasters. In this verse John echoes the teaching of Jesus (Jn 14:26; 16:13) and agrees with the declarations of Paul (1 Co 2:11-12) concerning the teaching ministry of the Holy Spirit.

John is not penning this epistle to those who "know not the truth" (2:21). In fact, quite the opposite is true. There are two basic facts which underlie his writing. First, he addresses them because they know the truth, and it is to this knowledge that he now appeals as he warns them against the threat of false teachers. Second, he writes because it is evident that "no lie is of the truth." That is, truth does not produce falsehood. This is a general principle, applicable to all truth and all falsehood, but John no doubt has in mind the more specific application to the truth of Christ's incarnation. That truth and the Gnostic denial of it are diametrically opposed and mutually exclusive. Since this is true, those who know the truth will naturally reject falsehood when it is presented to them, because they will recognize its contradiction of the truth.

Knowledge is always the most effective antidote for error. If we possess a genuine, firsthand knowledge of Christ and know, at least, the basic facts of the Christian faith, we will be able to recognize false teaching and to avoid its seductive snare.

THE CHRISTOLOGICAL TEST (2:22-23)

Negative statement (2:22-23a). Here, by means of a rhetorical question, John identifies the falsehood which he has in mind in verse 21. It is the denial "that Jesus is the Christ." The apostle's statement turns upon the meaning of the terms "Jesus" and "Christ." By the first he refers to the Man Jesus. On the other hand, the term "Christ," although it would normally refer to the Jewish Messiah, here reflects the Gnostic teaching which John is refuting. Cerinthus, who was a contemporary of John, taught that the divine Christ came upon the human Jesus at baptism and left Him just before His death. To the Cerinthian Gnostics the Man Jesus and the divine Christ were two separate and distinct beings. Jesus was not the God-Man possessing in the one person two natures, human and divine.

He who utters such a denial is "the liar" (Greek, *ho pseustēs*). This is the liar who surpasses all other liars. Furthermore, he is the "antichrist." By this the apostle John does not mean that he is the great, final Antichrist of the great tribulation period; he is, rather, one who is motivated by Antichrist's spirit which is at work in the present age (cf. 1 Jn 2:18; 4:3; 2 Th 2:7-8).

The denial is further explained as a repudiation of both "the Father and the Son." The term "Son" sheds light on John's use of the word "Christ." Rather than stressing the Hebrew concept of Messiahship, the apostle is speaking of the denial of Jesus' divine sonship.

In verse 23 he further explains the scope of such a denial. To deny that Jesus is the God-Man, the Son of God incarnate, is also to repudiate God the Father. It is not possible to reject Christ without rejecting God. Remember the words of Jesus: "No man cometh unto the Father, but by me" (Jn 14:6*b*). Therefore the Gnostic heresy was not a minor theological disagreement. It struck at the person of Christ, the very heart of the Christian faith, destroying the only way by which man can enter saving fellowship with God. The same is true of such modern counterparts of Gnosticism as Christian Science, Unity, New Thought, and Unitarianism, all of which deny the actual incarnation of the second Person of the Trinity.

Positive statement (2:23*b*). In contrast to the Gnostic denial and its terrible result, John briefly declares the result of confessing the truth concerning the person of Christ. The one who "acknowledgeth the Son" is brought into vital fellowship with God the Father. He "hath the Father also." In verses 22-23 the apostle has set forth the Christological test of fellowship with God. He who has entered the saving relationship of fellowship with God has confessed the truth of the incarnation: Jesus Christ is God's Son come in human flesh. On the other hand, the one who denies this central truth thereby reveals that he has no such saving relationship.

THE SECRET OF CONTINUING FELLOWSHIP (2:24-28)

Three facts are true of the person whose profession of saving fellowship is genuine. First, the truth will remain in the believer (2:24). Second, the anointing of the Holy Spirit indwells the believer (2:27). And third, the believer continues in vital relationship with Christ (2:24*b*, 27-28).

By that "which ye have heard from the beginning" (2:24), John is referring to the truth of the gospel, but with special emphasis on the incarnation. This truth was the traditional apostolic message which had been proclaimed "from the beginning," that is, from the time when the gospel was first brought to Asia by the apostle Paul (A.D. 53-55). (Cf. Ac 18:19; 19:10.) Now, some forty years later, John exhorts his readers to let that truth continue in them. In the face of the

Gnostic threat, they were to cling tenaciously to this wonderful message, not surrendering its precious reality nor compromising its purity in any way.

This is not mere stubborn allegiance to an ancient creed. In 2:24*b* the apostle explains that the one who possesses this truth "shall continue in the Son, and in the Father." In other words, the intimate, saving relationship which John describes as fellowship with God is only possible for the one who possesses the truth of the gospel. And the continuation of that relationship is dependent upon the continuing possession of the truth. The three English words "abide," "remain" and "continue" are all translations of the same Greek word *menō,* which speaks of continued dwelling.

This passage is reminiscent of Jesus' words in John 15 concerning the vine and the branches. There it is the one who abides in Christ who, rather than being cast out, bears much fruit.

At first glance verse 25 may seem to be a parenthetical statement with no direct bearing on the main thrust of the passage. Such, however, is not the case. The purpose of this verse is, no doubt, to show that the experience of continuing "in the Son, and in the Father" (2:24) is not a temporary abiding; instead, it is the possession of eternal life. Thus, to have fellowship with God (1:6-7), to be in Him (2:5), to abide in Him (2:6, 24, 27-28), and to have the Father and the Son (2:23) are all varying descriptions of the same experience, namely, eternal life. That this life was promised by Christ Himself is suggested by the emphatic *autos* ("he himself"). "This is the promise which he himself promised" (Greek) (cf. Jn 3:15; 4:14).

Anyone who professes to have such life can be put to the test to see if his profession is valid. In 1 John 1:5—2:11, John has described the ethical test. He who possesses eternal life will walk in the light (1:7), which includes obedience (2:3-6), confession of sin (1:8-10), and love for God's people (2:9-11). Here in 1 John 2:18-28 John sets forth the Christological test.

The person who possesses eternal life will hold to the truth
that Jesus is the Christ, God the Son come in human flesh
(2:22-23).

At this point (2:26) John explicitly declares his purpose in
writing. In their broadest sense these words may apply to the
whole epistle, but their most certain application is to the immediate context (2:18-28). What the author has been saying
about antichrists (2:18-19, 22), about "the liar" and the denial
that Jesus is the Christ (2:22) is in reality a warning against
the Gnostic seducers. The Greek present participle *planōntōn*
("deceive") does not mean that the false teachers were actually
seducing the believers. Instead this is a tendential use of the
present tense, indicating what the heretics intended to do. This
epistle is a warning against those who *would* lead believers
astray. The verb *planaō,* here translated "deceive," literally
means "to cause to go astray" and is used in Matthew 18:12 of
the sheep which wandered from the flock.

Although John's warnings were directed against an early
form of Gnosticism, they may be applied in principle to those
who propagate error in our day. Anyone who denies the truth
of the incarnation falls under John's condemnation, whether
his denial comes in the first century or the twentieth. In denying this one item of our faith he has denied the faith in its
entirety. If Jesus was not God in human flesh, His death has
no more saving value than that of any other good man. And
when the element of salvation is extracted from Christianity,
nothing remains but an empty shell.

Verse 27 begins with an emphatic contrast. Following his
warning against deceivers, John says, And as for you, "the
anointing which ye have received of him abideth in you." As
seen in 2:20, this is the Holy Spirit whom God imparts to the
believer at the time of his regeneration, not as a temporary
gift, but as One which continually indwells the Christian
(Greek present tense). The following clause seems to suggest
that the possession of the Spirit makes all human teachers un-
necessary. This, however, cannot be John's meaning, for he

himself was engaged in teaching, and the New Testament commends the office of teacher (Eph 4:11) and the gift of teaching (Ro 12:7). This statement must be understood in the light of its context and of the situation which called it forth. The Gnostic teachers were insisting that a higher form of knowledge must be added to the teaching of traditional Christianity. To this claim John replies, "Ye need not that any man teach you." What the indwelling Spirit had already taught them was perfectly adequate. It could not be superseded.

This teaching ministry of the Holy Spirit is not the actual impartation of facts. Instead it is the commending of truth to the regenerated mind, the impartation of the ability to receive and appreciate truth, the activity of making revealed truth meaningful to the believer. In reality the apostle is magnifying the ability of the Christian layman to understand spiritual truth with the aid of the Holy Spirit.

John's statement "Ye shall abide in him" (2:27b) is best understood as a command. The Spirit teaches us to abide in Christ and, as 2:24 indicates, this is fulfilled by allowing God's truth to remain in us. Thus our continuing in Christ is brought about by the abiding truth and the abiding Spirit. The perseverance of the believer is guaranteed by the Lord Himself (Jn 10:27-29). In unequivocal terms Christ declared, "They shall never perish." The other side of the coin, however, reveals that it is also true that the believer *does* persevere. He keeps on following Christ (Jn 10:27). His responsibility is to continue in Christ as the Holy Spirit teaches him (1 Jn 2:27). Thus while it is true that God guarantees our security, at the same time our regenerated wills are active in persisting in a saving relationship with the Lord.

The command to abide in Christ is repeated in 2:28 as John brings the first major section of his epistle to a close. He has viewed the Christian life as fellowship with God and has marked out two tests to ascertain the genuineness of fellowship. The first is the ethical test of walking in the light (1:5—2:11); the second is the doctrinal test of believing in the incarnation (2:18-28). The author then concludes, "And now, little children, abide in him." This is, in reality, a command to continue in the relationship of fellowship.

To this imperative is added a purpose for remaining in Christ, namely, that when He returns "we may have confidence, and not be ashamed." The word "confidence" (*parrēsian*) basically means "freedom of speech" and was used in secular Greek to express the freedom which was characteristic of a Greek democracy. Here the word signifies the bold confidence which is not inhibited by any sense of shame when we stand before the Lord at His coming. This confidence can only be the possession of those who are in Christ, that is, in a saving relationship to Him. Those who are not in the fellowship of the saved will "be ashamed before him at his coming." Literally John describes it as being ashamed *from* Him (Greek, *ap' autou*), which suggests a turning away from the Lord in shame. John uses the word *parrēsia* again in 3:21, 4:17 and 5:14. In Acts 4:29, 31 the same word appears, emphasizing boldness of speech in testifying for the Lord.

Second Cycle: The Christian Life Viewed as Divine Sonship (2:29—4:6)

In general the second cycle of John's epistle covers the same ground as the first. It is not, however, mere repetition. The subject is still the Christian life, but here it is represented as divine sonship rather than as fellowship with God. The same tests, the ethical (2:29—3:24) and the Christological (4:1-6), are set forth, but in each case the apostle advances beyond the previous cycle. New facets of each test are developed. Thus, both the Christian life and its tests are seen from a different point of view than they are in 1:5—2:28.

The key to this cycle is the concept of new birth. A Christian is a person who has been born of God and who thus bears the family likeness. The proverb "Like father, like son" is true of every member of God's family.

Sonship Tested on Ethical Grounds (2:29—3:24)

The ethical test of sonship is concerned with the practice of righteousness (2:29—3:10a) and the love of fellow believers (3:10b-24). Both elements will be present in the life of a child of God.

SONSHIP DEMANDS THE PRACTICE OF RIGHTEOUSNESS (2:29—3:10a)

The basic principle (2:29). John opens this second cycle of his epistle in the same way that he introduced the first cycle. He sets up the standard by which the genuineness of one's profession can be tested. In 1 John 1:5 the standard is God, who is declared to be light. That is, He is moral goodness—truth and holiness—and those who are in fellowship with Him will be like Him.

Here in 2:29 the standard is likewise God, who is described as righteous. Although the preceding verse obviously speaks of Christ, the pronoun "he" in verse 29 must refer to God the Father, because the verse goes on to say that the one who "doeth righteousness is born of him." The New Testament never speaks of being born of Christ. The Christian is born of God (1 Jn 3:9; 5:1) and is therefore a child of God (1 Jn 3:1-2, 10).

The point which John makes in verse 29 is that the son will be like the father. If God the Father is righteous, the child of God will manifest the same characteristic. Righteousness will be the habitual practice of his life (Greek present tense, *poiōn*), proving that he is born of God. This does not mean that every person who appears to be good is therefore a child of God. The epistle indicates that other characteristics must also be present. For example, the Christian believes that Jesus is the Christ, the Son of God (5:1, 5), and he loves God's people (5:1).

The privilege of sonship (3:1-3). In these three verses John pauses to marvel at the amazing love which condescends to call us "the sons of God" (3:1). Words cannot express the wonder which grips the apostle's soul. Lenski suggests that the word

"Behold" (Greek aorist imperative) means "Just take a look at." The expression "what manner of" reveals the astonishment which the author feels as he considers the love which lifts us from the position of guilty sinners to that of divine sonship. This love (*agapē*) is not the selfish, acquisitive love which is called forth by the desirability of the person who is loved. Instead *agapē* is the selfless, outgoing love which purposes to give itself even though its object may be unlovely.

The word translated "sons" in the Authorized Version is *tekna* ("children"), coming from the verb *tiktein* ("to bear"). We have entered God's family by the route of new birth. Something of the thrill which the thought of sonship produced is seen in additional words found in the earliest and best Greek manuscripts. It seems certain that John's original read, "Behold what manner of love the Father hath bestowed upon us, that we should be called the children of God, *and we are!*" Inasmuch as we are God's children we are like God's unique Son in that we are foreigners to this godless world ("the world knoweth us not") just as He was.

Divine sonship is a present reality, but it also has meaning for the future (3:2). "What we shall be" has not yet been fully revealed. However, John was sure of at least one fact concerning the future of God's children: "We shall see him [just] as [*kathōs*] he is." From this fact the apostle deduces that "we shall be like him." John does not say that we shall *become* like Him *because* we see Him just as He is. Rather, he says that because we know that we shall see Him, we also know that we shall be like Him. Only as we are like Him can we see Him.

When Christ comes again the process of sanctification will reach its consummation and the believer will be transformed morally so that sin no longer will dwell in him, nor will he commit sin anymore. Furthermore, the body will be changed so that it will never again be subject to death and decay. Thus, we shall be like Christ both bodily and morally. This is the future aspect of sonship. Because we are God's children today, we shall be like Christ when He comes again. The present-day reality of sonship becomes the guarantee of the future reality of perfect likeness to our Lord.

On the other hand, as we see in 2:3, there is a sense in which the future brings influence to bear upon the present. The hope to which John here refers is not said to be one which resides in the believer ("in him"); instead it is a hope which rests upon Christ (Greek, *ep' autô*). He is the foundation. The confident assurance of Christ's coming has a purifying effect upon the believer here and now. It sets in motion a process of purification (Greek, "keeps purifying") which molds the believer more and more into the likeness of Christ ("even as he is pure"). The concept of purity is one of freedom from the filth of sin. As Christ's life was one of moral cleanness, so the believer is to engage habitually in purging his life from sin.

Sonship, according to John, both in its present and its future aspects, is one of likeness to Christ and thus to God. The child of God, because he is born of God (2:29) and because he is possessed by a purifying hope (3:3), lives a life of righteousness and purity, thus identifying himself as a member of God's family.

The sign of sonship (3:4-10a). In 3:4-8 the apostle advances three reasons why sin is not compatible with the Christian life. The first concerns the nature of sin, which is described as lawlessness (3:4). The statement "Sin is the transgression of the law" is so structured that it actually equates the two items, thus making sin and lawlessness identical and interchangeable. Anyone who commits sin acts in defiance of God's holy law. Lawlessness does not refer to the mere ignorance of, or absence of, law; it speaks of action in direct opposition to law. Here, as in the succeeding verses of this section, John uses the Greek present tense verb when he speaks of committing sin. The kind of action normally portrayed by the present tense is continuing action. Thus the most literal translation of 3:4a is "Everyone who is practicing sin is also practicing lawlessness."

Inasmuch as sin is the violation of the law of God, it should not be a characteristic of God's child. It is inconsistent for a member of God's family, who should bear the family likeness, to practice sin. In so doing he would be denying the family likeness and repudiating God's will.

The second reason why sin is not compatible with the Christian life concerns the person and work of Christ (3:5-7). We are told that "he was manifested to take away our sins" (3:5a). The word "he" translates the demonstrative pronoun *ekeinos*, literally meaning "that one" and referring emphatically to Christ. John's statement concerns a truth well known to his readers. Since it is an indisputable fact that the purpose of Christ's incarnation was to destroy sin, it is obviously inconsistent for His followers to practice it. It may be that the apostle is speaking specifically of the sins of believers as the Authorized Version seems to suggest ("our sins"). Some Greek manuscripts have the first person pronoun *hēmōn* ("our"); better manuscripts, however, simply have the article *tas*. Even so, the translation "our sins" may be in order, for the Greek article is often used in a possessive sense. Thus, the case for sin's incompatibility is made even stronger if John is understood to be saying that Christ came to take away *our* sins. How great is the inconsistency if the believer should practice the very things which Christ came to destroy!

For this reason John says, "Whosoever abideth in him sinneth not" (3:6a). The person who "abideth in him" is the one who is saved as contrasted with the unsaved. He is the one who is in Christ, living in an eternal relationship with Him. John is not speaking only of the Christian who is living close to the Lord as contrasted with the Christian who is not as close to Him. Instead he is asserting that any person in Christ and thus savingly related to Christ "sinneth not" (see comment on 2:24-25, 27-28).

Does this mean that the believer does not commit sin? Such a statement would contradict other passages which indicate that the Christian does commit sin (1 Jn 1:8—2:2). An examination of the tense of the Greek verb, however, will dissolve the difficulty. *Hamartanei* is in the present tense and therefore depicts continuing action. John does not say that the one who abides in Christ does not commit a single act of sin, which would be expressed by a Greek aorist tense. Instead he declares, "No one [*pas . . . ouch*] who dwells in him is practicing sin." He may, and does, commit individual acts of sin, but he does not habitually live a life of sin. Why? Because sin is incompatible with the believer's position in Christ (cf. 3:4-5).

The opposite side of the coin is described in 3:6*b*. Anyone who habitually commits sin (present tense, *hamartanōn*) "hath not seen him, neither known him." Such a person obviously is not in saving relation to the Lord. He has never—even to this present moment (perfect tense, *heōraken*)—seen Him. This does not refer to vision with one's physical eyes, but rather to the spiritual sight of faith. And if we have not seen Him, we most certainly have never known Him (perfect tense, *egnōken*). Since this is the opposite of the previous statement, it is clear that John uses the expression "abideth in him" to describe the one who has both seen and known Christ and is thus saved. The general rule, then, is that the Christian does not habitually practice sin, and the person who does continually engage in sin has never come to a saving knowledge of the Lord.

A reminder of the occasion which led to the writing of this epistle is injected in 3:7: "Little children, let no man deceive you." This verse is introduced with the same term of endearment (*teknia,* "little born ones") as is found in 2:1. The deception referred to is pictured as the act of leading someone astray (see comment on 2:26). The particular area of possible deception with which John is here concerned is the area of practice. The heresy confronting John's readers was morally as well as doctrinally erroneous, for genuine knowledge (3:6*b*) will be accompanied by righteous living. Because the Gnostic claimed spiritual knowledge while living in sin, John insists that righteousness and knowledge of Christ cannot be divorced. "He that doeth righteousness is righteous, even as he [Christ] is righteous." In other words, he who knows Christ will be like Him. This means that since Christ is righteous, the believer will likewise be righteous. And the manifestation of this inner righteousness will be the believer's habitual practice of righteousness (present tense, *poiōn*). The life of the believer will be consistent with the life of Christ. There will be no incompatible practice of sin, so the family likeness will be apparent in the Christian's life.

The third reason why sin is incompatible with the Christian life is stated in 3:8: "He that committeth sin is of the devil" (see 3:4-5 for the first two reasons). Here again John is not speaking of committing a single act of sin. His present tense *poiōn* describes habitual practice. The person whose life is marked by such a practice is "of [*ek*] the devil." His source is Satan, which is to say that he is a child of the devil. Just as Christ is characterized by righteousness (3:7*b*), so the devil is engaged in the constant practice of sin. He "sinneth from the beginning." John cannot mean that the devil has eternally existed as a sinner, for Scripture knows only one eternal Being, God Himself. Nor can the apostle mean that in the beginning God created Satan as an evil being. God is most surely not the author of evil. The term "beginning" must refer to that period when all things had their beginnings, when sin entered the universe in the form of the first satanic rebellion against God (cf. Jn 8:44).

Since sin finds its source in the devil, it is manifestly inconsistent for the Christian to engage in its practice. This inconsistency is heightened by the reminder that Christ came to "destroy the works of the devil" (3:8*b*). Satan as the original sinner is the one who produces the deeds of sin which men commit. In the final analysis these are "the works of the devil." Inasmuch as the purpose of the incarnation was to destroy these works, they are most surely incompatible with the Christian life.

In 3:4-8 John has set forth reasons why sin is incompatible with the Christian life. In 3:9-10*a* he goes so far as to assert the impossibility of habitual sin. Again the Authorized Version's translation may lead one to understand John to be teaching some form of sinless perfection. "Whosoever is born of God doth not commit sin" (3:9*a*). However, as in 3:8, the verb is in the present tense and thus does not depict an individual act of sin but the continuing practice of sin. No one who has been born of God and now is a member of His family makes sin the habit of his life. That this is true of everyone who has been regenerated is made clear by the Greek construction (*pas . . . ou*, "no one").

The reason why this is true is that "his seed remaineth in him." The seed (*sperma*) is that element in the process of reproduction which carries both life and the family characteristics. To use modern scientific terminology, the sperm is a bearer of the genes, which transmit heredity. God's child does not engage in the continual practice of sin because, by reason of his spiritual heredity, this is contrary to his nature. In fact, John actually declares that "he cannot sin, because he is born of God" (3:9*b*). Again the present tense verb indicates that he cannot continue in habitual sin. The continuing practice of sin is contrary to the nature which the child of God inherits from his heavenly Father and thus is an impossibility for him.

It is apparent that there are two spiritual families (3:8-9), the family of God and the family of the devil (3:10). In the immediately preceding verses John has shown how the children of one family are to be distinguished from those of the other family. The members of God's family may be known by their characteristic practice of righteousness. No one who is not practicing righteousness is of (*ek*, "from") God. Since there are but two spiritual families, such a person is from the devil; that is, the devil is his father. Thus, in John's day when Gnosticism was beginning to make its claims to lofty spiritual knowledge (and in our day as well) a crucial test of the reality of one's Christian profession was the presence or absence of the practice of righteousness in one's life.

SONSHIP DEMANDS THE LOVE OF FELLOW BELIEVERS (3:10*b*-24)

The transition (3:10*b*). Almost imperceptibly the discussion passes from the practice of righteousness to the love of fellow believers. The Christian life is still being viewed as divine sonship and John is continuing to describe the two spiritual families of Satan and of God, but he now moves on to a second family characteristic. The negative phrase "neither he that loveth not his brother" directly asserts that one who does not love the people of God is not a member of God's family. Indirectly this phrase tells us two things: (1) he who does *not* love God's people is a member of the devil's family, and (2) he who *does* love God's people is a member of God's family.

The command to love (3:11). That the love of the Christian brotherhood is an essential part of the Christian life is shown by the fact that it has been commanded "from the beginning." Here, the use of the term "beginning" cannot refer to eternity past nor to creation, since such times obviously antedated John's readers by many centuries. What he has in mind must be the beginning of their Christian experience (cf. 2:1).

The teaching of the Gnostics was a later arrival upon the scene, but the command to love was a part of the primitive apostolic message. Apparently it was first imparted to the readers when Paul penetrated the province of Asia with the gospel almost forty years before (Ac 18:19; 19:1-41). In reality this command rests not merely upon apostolic authority but upon the word of Jesus Himself (Jn 13:34-35; 15:12, 17).

As in the discussion of righteousness (2:29—3:10*a*), the use of the present tense verb *agapōmen* ("love") is significant. It is the continuing attitude and practice of love which marks the life of the Christian. As in 2:9-11, John is not speaking of perfection in love, but of that which is generally true of the Christian. Although love is normally present, on occasion the believer may be less than loving (just as walking in the light did not preclude the necessity of confessing one's sins, 1:7—2:2).

Negative examples (3:12-13). An effective way to point up a desirable quality or practice is to contrast it with its opposite. This John does in verses 12-13, where two examples of hatred are set forth, the first of which is the prototype of the second. Cain is an early example of a person who is "of that wicked one" (v. 12). Physically he was a son of Adam, but spiritually and morally he was a child of the devil. This is no doubt suggested by the employment of the same word to describe the works of Cain as is used of the devil. Satan is designated as "that wicked one" (*ponērou*); Cain's deeds are called "evil" (*ponēra*). Christ declared that the devil "was a murderer from the beginning" (Jn 8:44). Thus, since Satan was his father, Cain followed in his footsteps and likewise became a murderer. The Greek word translated "slew" (*esphaxen*) literally means "to cut the throat," and in John's day had come to refer to any violent killing involving bloodshed.

John explains that Cain killed Abel "because his own works were evil, and his brother's righteous." Then as now the righteousness of the upright man reveals in stark contrast the sinfulness of the wicked man and, as a result, the latter hates the former. It is not that the wicked envy the righteous because they are righteous, but rather that they hate the righteous because their wickedness stands rebuked and condemned by the very presence of righteousness. Cain resented the fact that his brother's offering found acceptance with God while his own was rejected (Gen 4:1-8).

The second example of hatred is one that is contemporary with the reader (v. 13). The conditional clause "if the world hate you" seems to suggest merely the possibility of hatred. However, the Greek construction reveals that John took it for granted that the world *does* hate the believer. The clause may be paraphrased "since the world is hating you." The "world" is here to be understood as that organized system of evil which is set in opposition to God and His people (see 2:15-17).

Apparently this opposition had disturbed John's readers, for he urges them to stop marveling (Greek negative particle with the present tense imperative verb) because the world was hating them. The word "marvel" indicates astonishment caused by something which is viewed as a wonder or a mystery (cf. 1 Pe 4:12). The fact that the world hates God's people is really no mystery, for the world, like Cain, is "of that wicked one." Those who belong to the evil world system are members of the devil's family, and therefore they will reflect his attitude of hatred toward God's people. As then, so now godlessness is disturbed by the condemning presence of righteousness in its midst, and it would remove the cause of its discomfort if it could.

The love test (3:14-15). John turns now from the negative examples of hatred to the positive mark of love. The contrast is shown by the pronoun "we" (v. 14), which, because of its emphatic position in the sentence may be paraphrased "but as for us." The world is characterized by hatred but, as for us, we are marked by love. Although God most assuredly desires Christians to love the people of the world, John is here speaking specifically of love for the members of God's family. "The brethren" are those who have the same spiritual Father as we have (cf. 5:1). It is this family love for those who, like us, have been regenerated that is a proof "that we have passed from death unto life." From 2:9-11 the reader may deduce that love for fellow believers is evidence that one has been saved, whereas hatred is proof that one is still in the darkness of sin. Here in 3:14, however, this fact is explicitly stated. Loving the brethren is proof that we are no longer spiritually dead but now have eternal life (cf. v. 15).

That John does not have in mind a momentary flash of affection is evident from the use of the Greek present tense, meaning "we are loving." Love for God's people is the habitual practice of our lives. Furthermore, the use of the verb *agapaō* ("love") shows that the author is speaking of that selfless outgoing attitude toward others which is not bent on acquiring for oneself but on giving. *Agapē* is not overwhelmingly emotional. Although emotion is involved, the intellectual and volitional elements are significantly present. We love our brother in Christ, not because he is lovable in himself, but because we know that he is our brother and because God has commanded that we love him.

However, just as it is true that the presence of love for fellow believers is evidence of eternal life, it is likewise true that the absence of love is the indication that one is spiritually dead. The person who is not loving "abideth in death," that is, he remains in the state in which he was born, dead in trespasses and sins (Eph 2:1) .

The closing words of verse 14 are a strong statement to which some may take exception. Therefore, John proceeds in verse 15 to demonstrate its validity. His declaration that "whosoever hateth his brother is a murderer" is a restatement of the teaching of Jesus in Matthew 5:21-22. Sin is not primarily the overt act; it is basically the inner attitude (cf. Mt 5:27-28) . Hatred, then, is not to be viewed as a harmless attitude of mind, nor merely an aversion toward someone. Hatred is the desire to do away with a person. There may be neither sufficient courage nor adequate opportunity to fulfill this desire, but hatred wishes to be rid of him nevertheless. Thus, hatred is the brutal cold poison which is the prime ingredient of murder.

The generally accepted truth ("and ye know") upon which John builds his argument is that "no murderer hath eternal life abiding in him." This does not mean that a person who has committed a murder cannot afterward trust Christ and receive life eternal. What John is pointing to as fact is that no one who has been born again and thus possesses eternal life will commit murder. He takes it for granted that for a man to murder clearly proves that he is not saved. Thus, since hatred is to be equated with murder, the one who hates is also devoid of eternal life.

The test of love (3:16-18) . In verses 14-15 love is declared to be a test by which it can be determined whether or not a person is saved. Now John moves on from the love test to the test of love. The question in verses 16-18 is How can one tell whether or not a person's love is genuine? If there is no sure way of recognizing genuine love, then the love test loses its value.

However, John declares that there is a way by which we can know genuine love when we see it. "Hereby [by this] perceive we the love" (v. 16). Note that the italicized words "of God" are not found in the original text. The definite article before the noun "love" (*tēn agapēn*) identifies the particular love which John has in mind. It is that love of which he has been speaking in the immediately preceding context, the love which is described by the word *agapē*, whether it appears in God or in man (see comment on v. 14). This love is known by the expression of itself in overt action. We know that Christ loved us "because he laid down his life for us."

Not only does His act of love prove the reality of His love, but it provides a pattern for us. If our love for our brothers in Christ is genuine, "we ought to lay down our lives" for them when it is needful.

In verse 17 the same truth is set forth negatively. John sets forth the hypothetical case of a person who "hath this world's good." He has those things that are necessary for the support of physical life in this world. There is no indication that he is wealthy, but only that he does have something which he can share. Furthermore, he is well aware of his brother's continuing need (Greek present tense). In fact, his awareness is likewise a continuing experience (Greek present tense). He apparently witnesses repeatedly the evidence of the need. But, as Robertson graphically explains, he slams shut the door of his compassions.[6] The word *kleisēi* ("shutteth up") is in the aorist tense, indicating point action in contrast to the linear action depicted in the three preceding verbal forms in this verse. The Authorized Version's "bowels of compassion" (*splagchna*) is comparable to our word *heart* when used as the seat of the emotions.

John's question "How dwelleth the love of God in him?" is in reality a denial that God's love is dwelling in such a person. Inasmuch as the context is dealing with love for men rather than God, the love of God here must be the love of which God is the Author and source and which has men for its object.

Such love, if present, will express itself in overt acts of love; it cannot be hidden. Genuine love gives to those in need; it willingly sacrifices itself for the one who is loved. Thus, it is more than words, and more than mere sentiment; it is the expression of the whole man—intellect, emotions and will—acting in behalf of one's fellow man. And it is only this genuine love that acts which constitutes proof that "we have passed from death unto life" (v. 14). Any Gnostic claim to love God's people would appear hollow and empty when submitted to this acid test.

John concludes this section on the test of love (3:16-18) with a practical exhortation addressed to his "little children." This term is a reminder of their spiritual birth by virtue of which they are all members of God's family. The exhortation in true Johannine style is first put negatively and then positively. God's people are not to "love in word, neither in tongue," that is, they are not to love with word nor with the tongue. This suggests that love is not to be merely a matter of speech, merely the meaningless exercise of the tongue. Instead we are to love "in deed and in truth." As verses 16-17 indicate, love is to be a matter of action. In fact, the necessary expression of genuine love is loving action. Love which expresses itself only in verbalization is not real love at all.

However, since even acts which seem to be motivated by love may be hypocritical, John adds the words "in truth." Our love must be characterized by reality rather than by sham or pretense, for nothing less than genuine love is sufficient to prove that a person has "passed from death unto life" (v. 14).

The fruits of love (3:19-24). In this section the author discusses two products which issue from genuine love: assurance (vv. 19-20) and answered prayer (vv. 21-24).

The word "hereafter" (v. 19) clearly refers back to the kind of love to which John exhorts his readers in verse 18, that is, love which acts and which is genuine. When our lives manifest such love "we know that we are of the truth." This is a firm knowledge which rests not on our feelings but on the

presence in our lives of that which is not natural to the unre-
generate. We can see there the habit of self-sacrificial sharing
with brothers who are in need. The fact that such love is not
mere human love indicates that God is at work in our hearts,
and thus we can be sure that we are "of the truth." This prepositional phrase literally means that truth is the source from
which we have come. Our spiritual experience springs from
the truth of God rather than from error. We are thus proved
to be the people of God.

The second half of verse 19 implies that the Christian's heart
may at times be stricken with uncertainty and insecurity. It
may engage in self-condemnation. John uses the term "heart"
to refer to the whole inner man, but he especially has in mind
the conscience and the feelings. When such feelings of insecurity and self-condemnation begin to plague the believer,
he may calm his disturbed heart by considering the evidence in
his life of genuine love which is willing to sacrifice and share
with those in need. The word "assure" literally means "to
persuade." In this way the condemning heart can be persuaded
that it is "of the truth," and thus of God.

The Greek of verse 20 is somewhat obscure, probably because
the author has omitted a word which he assumes his readers
will naturally supply. The verse is made up of two dependent
clauses: (1) "For if our heart condemn us"; and (2) "God is
greater than our heart, and knoweth all things." Perhaps the
best solution is to assume that John expected his readers to
supply something like "it is evident." Thus, the verse would
read, "For if our heart condemn us, *it is evident* God is greater
than our heart, and knoweth all things."

The human heart, even of a regenerated person, is not in-
fallible. It may subject one to the most agonizing feelings of
condemnation and insecurity. God, on the other hand, being
omniscient, never misjudges a situation. He assures us that the
presence of self-sacrificing, self-giving love in a person's life is
certain evidence that he is born of God. The fruit of love, then,
for the believer who has a sensitive conscience is assurance.

John does not suggest that we look for assurance to any ritual, such as baptism; or any affiliation, such as church membership. He does not even call upon us to remember a moment of decision when we consciously professed faith in Christ as Saviour, as important as such an act may be. In this passage the assurance of salvation is based upon a work which is occurring in the believer's life. It is not that we earn our salvation and thus can be sure of it; instead it is that our salvation manifests its reality through the presence of the love of God in our redeemed lives.

The second fruit of love is answered prayer (3:21-24). This will be found in the life of the believer whose heart no longer condemns him (v. 21). Love banishes self-condemning insecurity and in its place leaves "confidence toward God." *Parrēsian* ("confidence") was used in secular Greek to mean "freedom of speech." It carries both the ideas of boldness and of confidence. However, there is nothing of impropriety or brashness in the word. The one who is sure that he is born of God can come into God's presence without doubt or fear, there to speak freely and with confidence. He knows, because of love in his life, that he has been accepted by God and thus can be perfectly at ease in His presence. The Christian who possesses such assurance can "come boldly unto the throne of grace" (Heb 4:16), not as a guilty sinner, but rightfully as a child to his father.

However, the blessing of assurance involves not merely the believer's privilege of approaching God fearlessly, but a guarantee that his prayer will be answered. "Whatsoever we ask, we receive of him" (v. 22). This experience of asking and receiving is described with present tense verbs, indicating that it is the habitual pattern of life for the Christian. Asking is not a rare or spasmodic activity, but one which is carried on regularly; receiving likewise is not merely occasional, but a constantly repeated occurrence.

It must be recognized, however, that this statement is no blank check with which we can obtain anything we desire, regardless of what it is. There are other conditions in Scripture which govern prayer. An example is found in 5:14-15, where John explains that prayer, if it is to be answered, must be in accord with the will of God. The same idea, no doubt, may be inferred from the latter part of 3:22. The reason why God answers the prayer spoken of here is that "we keep his commandments, and do those things that are pleasing in his sight." Such a person is concerned with God's will, and his petitions will be in accord with that will.

Here again the present tense verbs "keep" and "do" are significant. The obedience which is a necessary condition for answered prayer is an habitual practice. Although the two expressions—"keep his commandments" and "do those things that are pleasing"—are essentially the same, the emphasis of each is different. Whereas commandments are binding requirements, the reference to things pleasing to God does not stress legal demand but glad and willing service.

In verse 23 the plural commandments become singular: "And this is his commandment." As Christ employed two great commandments to summarize all of the law and prophets (Mt 22:36-40), John now combines all of God's commands given to believers in this one imperative: "that we should believe . . . and love." In the mind of the writer these comprise but one commandment. Lenski explains, "You cannot believe without loving nor love without believing."[7] And Paul draws a contrast between ceremonial works and "faith which worketh by love" (Gal 5:6b). This two-pronged commandment deals with our relationship to God ("believe") and to man ("love"). Furthermore, it parallels the two basic tests which John establishes in this epistle, the Christological ("believe") and the ethical ("love"). The command is to "believe on the name," by which we understand John to mean that we are to believe all that the name signifies—divine sonship and real humanity combined in one Person, "his Son Jesus Christ." To this confession of faith no Gnostic could subscribe.

The better Greek texts show the verb "believe" to be in the

aorist tense, which stresses point action; whereas "love" is in the present tense, thus depicting a continuing practice. The point action is, no doubt, the initial act of confessing Christ as Saviour. In contrast to that once-for-all commitment, the believer is to show love to his Christian brothers as long as he lives. The clause "as he gave us commandment" reminds us of the new commandment which Christ gave to His disciples at the time of the last supper (Jn 13:34-35).

The plural "commandments" (v. 24) takes us back to verse 22, where it is clear that John is speaking of the commandments of God the Father. Furthermore, he retraces what he has said in 2:3-6 about obedience to God's commands and abiding in Him.

The continual keeping (Greek present tense) of God's commandments is evidence of a mutual indwelling. The person who thus obeys "dwelleth in him," that is, in God; by the same token God is shown to be indwelling the believer. The two are in mystical union with one another. The obedience described in verses 22-23 is impossible for mere human ability; consequently its presence in a person's life is clear evidence of a unique and intimate relationship with God. God dwells in him, and he dwells in God.

Many understand the word "hereby" (v. 24b) to refer not to what precedes but to what follows, namely, "the Spirit which he hath given us." However, it should be noted that both the words "hereby" and "by" occur in the Authorized Version. The first time it is the translation of the Greek preposition *en*, which is obviously instrumental in sense. The second occurrence of the word translates the preposition *ek*, which speaks of source. Thus, we may paraphrase John's statement as follows: "And by this means, that is, by the keeping of God's commandments, we know that He is indwelling us, and this assurance comes to us from the Holy Spirit whom God has imparted to us." Our assurance, therefore, is not arrived at merely by a process of reasoning. It comes to us from the Spirit as a part of the spiritual understanding which we are told to expect

from Him (see Jn 14:26; 16:13; 1 Co 2:9-12; 1 Jn 2:20, 27).
The Holy Spirit uses our obedience to the commandments—
our love of fellow believers "in deed and in truth"—to impart
the sure knowledge that we are in vital, saving union with God.

SONSHIP TESTED ON CHRISTOLOGICAL GROUNDS (4:1-6)

In verses 1-6 John advances his second statement of the
Christological test. The first discussion of this test is found in
2:18-28 where the Christian life is viewed as being intimate fellowship with God. In 2:29—4:6, however, the Christian life is
described as being divine sonship (3:1-2, 10). The believer is
born of God (2:29; 3:9). Although the expression "born of
God" does not occur in 4:1-6, the concept is present in this section. The phrase "of God" (*ek tou theou*) occurs six times in
these six verses. The Greek preposition *ek* speaks of source,
literally meaning "out of." Thus, the believer is "out of God."
God is his source; he is born of God. One test of the reality of
that birth is a person's attitude toward the person of Christ.

A WARNING AGAINST FALSE PROPHETS (4:1)

It is in verses like verse 1 that the urgent occasion for the
epistle is most clearly seen. John writes to believers, as is evident from the declaration of verse 4 as well as from the term
"beloved" (v. 1). However, there is indication that they have
been gullible when confronted with the claims of false teachers.
John's Greek construction shows that he is urging his readers
to stop believing "every spirit." They had naïvely been assuming the genuineness of every teacher who claimed to be from
God.

Thus, John commands, "Try the spirits whether they are of
God." The word "try" (*dokimazete*) was the technical term
for the testing of persons for public office. It should be the
continuing practice (Greek present tense) of the believer to
put spiritual leaders to the test to determine whether or not
they are doctrinally qualified for leadership.

John's use of the term "spirit" in this section is somewhat

unusual. However, it is to be noted that he is speaking of prophets, as the last part of the verse indicates. The biblical concept of a prophet is that he is a man who speaks under a supernatural inspiration. It was the coming of the Spirit of God upon Saul that enabled him to prophesy (1 Sa 10:6, 10). John's concept of a false prophet is that he is inspired by a false spirit which he designates as the "spirit of antichrist" (1 Jn 4:3). Thus, so closely does he identify the prophet and the spirit which inspires the prophet that he speaks not of the prophet but of the spirit, the real author of the prophet's message.

THE CHRISTOLOGICAL TEST (4:2-3)

John now proceeds to explain how to test the spirits. Because of the nature of the heresy which threatened his readers, the criterion to be used of necessity concerned the person of Christ. The test is first applied with positive (v. 2) and then with negative results (v. 3).

The positive statement (4:2). In a day when the Gnostic Cerinthus was spreading his destructive heresy abroad, how could Christian people discern which teachers came from God? John's answer is that any person who is from God will gladly confess "that Jesus Christ is come in the flesh." The Authorized Version's translation "confesseth not *that* Jesus Christ is come" suggests that the confession of a proposition *about* Jesus is intended. However, there is no word for "that" in the Greek text of verse 2. The confession is a confession of Jesus as a person rather than a confession of a proposition about the Person. John is not talking about the acceptance of a creed, but about faith in a Person who has become and still is incarnate (Greek perfect tense). The best translation of verse 2*b* is "Every spirit who is confessing Jesus as Christ come in the flesh is of God." Such a person believes that the human Jesus and the divine Christ are one and the same Person—God incarnate. The person who makes such a confession does so under the motivation of the Spirit of God, and his declaration indicates that he "is of God" (cf. 5:1).

John does not intend to suggest that the fact of the incarnation is the only important doctrine and that all other doctrines are insignificant. The nature of the heresy being combatted—Cerinthianism, with its perverted Christology—demanded that the criterion for testing be Christological.

The negative statement (4:3). This verse was aimed specifically at the Gnostic heresy of Cerinthus, who apparently lived in Ephesus concurrently with John. He taught that Jesus was a mere human being, born by natural procreation, and that the divine element, the Christ, came upon Him at His baptism (cf. Mt 3:16) and left Him just before His death (cf. Mt 27:46). Thus the divine did not become intimately involved with sinful human flesh; it only rested *upon* the human Jesus. Consequently the test of the incarnation, which is stated in verse 2, clearly indicated that Cerinthus was "not of God," for he refused to confess belief in Jesus as the incarnate Christ.

Such a denial is motivated not by the Spirit of God but by the "spirit of antichrist." This does not imply that the Antichrist was already in existence in the first century. However, the spirit which will be characteristic of Antichrist when he comes was then active and still is. As the Spirit of God is personal (v. 2), so the spirit of Antichrist is personal. It, no doubt, is in reality the spirit of Satan himself. Revelation 13:2 informs us that when the great end-time opponent of Christ appears, Satan will give him his power, his throne and great authority.

The Christological test is equally applicable in our day, especially when one is confronted with such current Gnostic cults as Christian Science, New Thought, the Unity School of Christianity, and the Theosophical Society. The test may also be applied to anyone who denies the deity of Jesus. He who strikes at the incarnation strikes at the very heart of the Christian faith. If Jesus was not both God and Man He could not be our Saviour. In order to die in our place, it was necessary that He become man; in order for His death to have infinite value, He must be God.

Religious teachers may be judged on the basis of what they say about the person of Christ (4:1-3), but they may also be judged on the basis of their listeners (4:4-6). We can tell whether or not they are of God by examining the persons who hear them.

This section is marked by strong contrasts between those who are "of God" and those who are "of the world." In contrast to those who deny the incarnation (v. 3), John opens verse 4 with the declaration "As for you, you are of God" (free trans.). The personal pronoun "ye" is emphatic, as are the pronouns "they" and "we" in verses 5 and 6. John has no doubt that his readers are "of God," for they confess Jesus as Christ come in flesh (v. 2). The phrase "of God" speaks of source and thus is almost the same as "born of God" (cf. 2:29; 3:9).

Furthermore, John's readers were victorious over the false prophets who were denying the incarnation. They had not been led astray by blasphemous claims, because they possessed sufficient inner resources to overcome. The expressions "he that is in you" and "he that is in the world" no doubt refer to the Spirit of God on the one hand and the spirit of Antichrist or Satan on the other hand. Satan is powerful and his delusion is dangerous, but the Spirit of God, who indwells every child of God, is the omnipotent Spirit of truth before whom no delusion can stand.

In sharp contrast, the false teachers "are of the world" (v. 5). They do not come from God but from the evil system which is organized against God, of which Satan is the prince (Jn 12:31). Because they come, spiritually and morally, from this evil world system, "therefore speak they of the world." By this the apostle does not mean that they are talking *about* the world, but rather that their message, like themselves, finds its source in the world. It springs from a secular, anti-Christian orientation. The result is that the people of the world listen to such a message. We may call this the hearing test. A religious teacher is to be identified by those who are interested in what he has to say. This is the old proverb in action on the spiritual plane: "Birds of a feather flock together."

The same principle applies to God's people as well. Verse 6 begins with a strong contrast: "But as for us, we are of God" (free trans.). Since our source is God (we are born of God), our message likewise comes from God, and therefore "he that knoweth God heareth us." God's messengers are marked by the fact that God's people are the ones who are listening (Greek present tense) to them. On the other hand, they are identified by those who do not listen to them. "He that is not of God" does not possess the spiritual orientation to be able to appreciate what God's messengers are saying.

Thus in 4:1-6 John has pointed out two tests by which it is possible to distinguish between the false prophets and the true. One is the content of their message: Do they confess Jesus as God's Son come in human flesh? The other test is the nature of their followers: Who listens to them? The people of God, or the people of the world? This is John's method of distinguishing "the spirit of truth" from "the spirit of error."

With this section John concludes his second cycle of thought in which he has viewed the Christian life as divine sonship. He who has been born of God will be marked by certain discernible characteristics, some of which are ethical in nature and some doctrinal. The member of God's family will possess righteousness, not sin, as the outstanding feature of his life (2:29—3:10*a*). His attitude toward God's people will be one of Godlike love expressing itself in explicit acts of sharing and self-sacrifice (3:10*b*-24). And finally, the person who is born of God will be one who confesses Jesus as God come in human flesh. To him the people of God will gladly listen (4:1-6).

Third Cycle: The Christian Life Viewed as the Interweaving of the Ethical and the Doctrinal (4:7—5:12)

This final cycle of the epistle is primarily characterized by an interweaving of themes from previous cycles into a single fabric of truth. In 1:5—4:6 John has set forth ethical and doctrinal tests by which the genuineness of a person's salvation can be ascertained. He has stressed love for fellow believers (2:7-11; 3:10b-24), obedience of divine commands (2:3-6; 3:22-23), and belief in Jesus as the Christ, the Son of God (2:22-23).

Now in 4:7—5:12 he shows that these are not qualities which may be possessed separately. They are all integrally related. No one item by itself can serve as a valid test of one's salvation. Belief must be accompanied by love and obedience, for love can only be produced by regeneration, and regeneration comes only as a result of belief. And obedience is the inevitable result of love.

THE ETHICAL ASPECT (4:7—5:5)

Whereas in the preceding cycles John has included both love and obedience or the practice of righteousness under the ethical test, in this concluding cycle the ethical section deals almost exclusively with love. It will be noted that the discussion is no mere repetition of 2:7-11 and 3:10b-24. Rather, the apostle now proceeds to explain how it is that love can be a test of one's possession of eternal life. He explains why it is that the believer will, as a fact, love his brothers in the faith.

THE SOURCE OF LOVE (4:7-16)

Love, the essence of God (4:7-8). John begins this final discussion of love for fellow believers by appealing to his readers as "Beloved" (v. 7), thus exemplifying that which he exhorts of them. His plea is that we should continually (Greek present tense) "love one another." Here, as elsewhere in 1 John, the author has in mind the love for fellow Christians. The exhortation is followed by a two-pronged reason. (1) "Love is of God." By using the article with "love" (*hē agapē*) the apostle makes it clear that he is talking of a particular love, the self-giving love which is characteristic of God, rather than love in general. This kind of love comes "from" (*ek*) God. (2) "Every one that loveth is born of God, and knoweth God." Since love comes from God, John can declare that the practice of love proves that a person has been "born of God" and knows God. It is only as we become God's children that this kind of love is possible for us. This verse, then, is an exhortation to believers to practice love toward each other because they are born again and they know God and thus are divinely enabled to exercise God's kind of love.

Just as the habitual practice of Christian love proves that a person knows God, so the failure of a person to exhibit such love demonstrates that he "knoweth not God" (v. 8). The tense of the verb "knoweth" is aorist, indicating that he has never come to know God. He has never known anything other than estrangement from his Maker.

And this is true because "God is love." In these three words lies the reason why children of God must, and do, love one another. John does not say that God loves or that God is loving, but that God *is* love. God in His essence is love. This is not to say that love is God, for the Greek construction will not allow such a meaning. Nor is this to suggest that God is merely a sentimental, soft-hearted, grandfatherly type who condones man's sin rather than punishing it. First John 1:5 also declares that "God is light," which is tantamount to saying that God is holiness. And love does not cancel holiness, nor holiness love. Robert Law, speaking of the nature of God, says, "That nature is *holy love*."[8]

This explains why a person who has been born of God must and will love with God's kind of love. The regenerated person has God's seed within him (1 Jn 3:9); he is a partaker of the divine nature (2 Pe 1:4); he is indwelt by God (1 Jn 3:24; 1 Co 6:19). Thus, since God who is love indwells the believer, love itself indwells the believer; therefore, love is a valid test of whether or not a person is born of God.

Christ, the manifestation of God's love (4:9-11). The apostle now turns from a discussion of the essential nature of God to the manifestation of that nature. God's love was manifested "toward us" (Greek, "among us") in the sending of "his only begotten Son" (v. 9). The term "only begotten" speaks of the uniqueness of the Son. Christ is God's *only* Son; there is no other. This helps us to understand the price that divine love was willing to pay. Our appreciation is heightened by the statement that God sent His Son "into the world," that evil order of things which is set in hateful opposition to God. Further understanding of His love is provided by the purpose of Christ's coming: "that we might live through him." His love was selfless and self-giving. He sacrificed Himself that those who are dead in sin might receive eternal life.

Lest anyone presume that the love of which John speaks is of human origin, and thus is something of which we may boast, he declares, "Herein is love" (v. 10). It is not in *our* love for God but in *His* love for us. The position of the Greek negative, the insertion of the personal pronouns "we" and "he," and the strong adversative conjunction "but" point up the forceful contrast which John uses to insist that this love of which he speaks is from God and Him alone. The nature of this love is seen in that it was spontaneous. Our love did not call it forth; it was self-initiated. As a result of it, He "sent his Son to be the propitiation for our sins."

The word "propitiation" is a technical term used in connection with sacrifices offered to a deity. Some commentators prefer to translate *hilasmon* as *expiation* rather than *propitiation* because they see in the latter term the pagan concept of appeasing the pettiness of an offended deity. Although it is true the term may be used in a pagan context, that is no reason why the pagan concept of God should be transported into the Christian context. The God of the Bible is a holy God, the moral Governor of His creation, whose righteousness has been violated by man's sin. Therefore, because He is a God of justice, He must demand the payment of sin's penalty. However, the God of justice is, at the same time, the God of love, and thus He Himself provided the payment in the propitiatory sacrifice of His Son.

"Herein is love"! God's kind of love gives an only Son to pay the penalty demanded by His justice. God's kind of love is not elicited by our love for Him; instead it is called forth by our sin and our need.

From this moving description of the manifestation of God's love, the apostle concludes that "we ought also to love one another" (v. 11). Again he reminds his readers that they are "beloved," perhaps referring not only to his love for them but to the fact that they are loved by God. There is no doubt in John's mind about the love of God. The condition "if God so loved" does not refer to a doubtful or hypothetical situation. It is the Greek simple condition which assumes the reality of its premise. It is the equivalent of saying, "since God so loved us."

The fact of God's matchless love lays upon us a continuing obligation (Greek present tense) to be loving one another. Not only is it true that we have received the nature of God by reason of our new birth and thus we should love, but we have the example of His love teaching us and persuading us to love each other. The words "so" and "also" are significant. The first gathers together all of the characteristics of divine love as John has described them in verses 9-10. The word "also" lays upon us the responsibility for manifesting similar characteristics. We are to love with Godlike love.

Love, the evidence of divine indwelling (4:12-13). John continues to explain the source of love. In verse 12 he argues from the fact that "no man hath seen God at any time." Since God is a Spirit (Jn 4:24), physical eyes cannot see Him. It is true that there have been theophanies such as the occasion when Moses saw the back of God (Ex 33:21-23), but what Moses saw was not God Himself (cf. v. 20) but a body which He assumed in order to appear to Moses. God in His essence cannot be seen by human eyes.

Nevertheless, it is possible to see the essential nature of God. This is not double talk; it is what John is saying in the remainder of verse 12. God in His essence is love, and we can see that love as it manifests itself through those in whom He dwells. "If we love one another," it is because God is indwelling us. This Godlike love for the members of God's family can only be explained by the fact that God, who is love, is present in the lives of those who manifest such love. When we love one another, "his love is perfected in us." Note that it is His love, not ours, which is perfected in us when we love each other. Thus, our love is in reality His love. When we love, it is God loving through us. Even the love which we seem to exercise finds its source in God.

The statement concerning perfected love does not mean that we ever attain to perfect love in this life. Only God is capable of flawless love. As in 2:5, John is saying that the love of God has reached its goal when it is manifested in the life of the believer. It is God's aim to produce His love in our lives. When we love one another this aim is accomplished and His love has reached the state of completeness in us.

In 1 John the word "hereby" usually refers to that which follows it rather than what precedes it (cf. 2:3; 3:16; 4:2). Its use here in verse 13 seems to be no exception. "Hereby"— that "he hath given us of his Spirit"— "know we that we dwell in him, and he in us." In verse 12 love for one another is evidence of God's indwelling; in verse 13 the presence of the Spirit is evidence of the same fact. These two proofs, love and the Holy Spirit, are really not independent of each other, for Paul reveals that love is produced in the believer's life by God the Spirit.

It is with purpose that John says "he hath given us *of* his Spirit" rather than "he hath given us *his Spirit*." When the New Testament refers to the giving or receiving of the Spirit as a person, the word "Spirit" occurs as direct object of the

verb (cf. Jn 20:22; Ac 8:15; 10:47; 15:8). Here, however, the
phrase "of [*ek*, "from"] his Spirit" indicates that God gives His
Spirit by measure to men. Only Christ received the Spirit without measure (Jn 3:34).

Divine indwelling, the result of faith (4:14-16). In these
verses the author begins that process of interweaving so characteristic of the third cycle of the epistle. In the midst of his
discussion of love, he moves almost imperceptibly to the subject of belief. His purpose seems to be to show the relationship
of these two qualities in the Christian's life.

The words "And we have seen and do testify" remind us of
1:1-2. The emphatic "we" no doubt refers to the eyewitnesses
of Christ's life on earth—to John and the other apostles. As in
1:1, the author speaks of careful and deliberate seeing. The
perfect tense indicates that what was seen still lingers in the
mind's eye. The fact that "the Father sent the Son to be the
Saviour of the world" is a continuing reality in his conscious-
ness. Consequently, he is continually bearing witness (Greek
present tense) to this most significant fact. That Christ came
to be "the Saviour of the world" leaves no room for a limited
atonement. His salvation was not intended for the elect only,
but for all of lost humanity.

In verse 14 John has advanced the testimony of a careful eyewitness to establish the historicity of the fact that "the Father
sent the Son to be the Saviour." Because this fact is true, the
confession that "Jesus is the Son of God" (v. 15) has significance. In reality this is John's Christological test by which we
can discern who is from God and who is not. To use the terminology of 4:2-3, the test has to do with the acceptance or rejection of the incarnation.

Cerinthus, the Gnostic teacher of John's day, could not make
such a confession, for to him Jesus was mere man and nothing
more. However, anyone who does confess the sonship of Jesus
shows that "God dwelleth in him, and he in God." Such a
confession of necessity is more than mental assent to a historical
fact. It is confession of trust in the incarnate Son as one's

Saviour. He who makes such a confession demonstrates that he is involved in the most intimate relationship with God. This mutual indwelling, however, is more than close fellowship. God in actual fact indwells the believer's person. Thus, divine indwelling and belief in the incarnate Son of God are integrally and inseparably related. The significance of this necessary relationship becomes apparent in the following verse.

The first person plural pronoun "we" (v. 16) refers not to John and the apostles, as in verse 14, but to John and his readers. Since the words "to us" (v. 16) most naturally include the readers, the pronoun "we" must refer to the same persons.

We may at first glance assume that the more exact order would be belief and knowledge, but John seems to reverse this order: "We have known and believed." More thorough consideration, however, reveals that there is good reason for this seeming reversal. "We have known" speaks of the understanding of spiritual truth, whereas "believed" describes the aspect of confidence in and conviction concerning that which is known. Spiritual perception leads to heartfelt conviction. Both verbs, being in the perfect tense, speak of the continuing state of understanding and conviction to which the believers have come.

The object of this knowledge and belief is "the love that God hath to us" (Greek, "in us"). Many commentators have struggled with this seemingly strange prepositional phrase. However, if we understand it in the light of the context, it is most reasonable to interpret it as referring to God's love which is in us (cf. v. 12, "his love is perfected *in us*").

This is borne out by the remainder of verse 16. Here John returns to his statement of verse 8, "God is love." Since God is love, to dwell in love is to dwell in God, and to be indwelt by love is to be indwelt by God. Thus, the apostle is repeating what he implies in verse 12. Christian love is God's love in the believer. In fact, it is God Himself indwelling the believer. And who is it who is indwelt but he who confesses "that Jesus is the Son of God" (v. 15). Thus in verses 14-16 the apostle has succeeded in showing that love and belief are knit together in an inseparable relationship.

The gist, then, of verses 7-16 is that God Himself is the source of Christian love. Since God, who is love, indwells the believer, the believer must and will love his fellow believers. Thus, love for the family of God is a valid test of one's salvation. If we have been born again, love will of necessity be present in our lives. If it is not, this is an indication that we have not been regenerated.

THE FRUIT OF LOVE (4:17-19)

The benefit which is derived from love is described from the positive point of view in verse 17 and from the negative in verse 18. John then rounds off the section by showing that God is the ultimate source of love, and therefore of assurance (v. 19).

Positive statement (4:17). A literal translation of the first clause of this verse would read: "In this is love perfected with us" (RSV). It is best to refer "in this" to the preceding statement. It is in the experience of dwelling in God and He in us (v. 16) that "the love" (the Godlike love which John has been describing) has been "perfected with us" (v. 17, RSV). This is not to say our love reaches perfection in this life. Instead, the love of which God is the Author reaches its goal as it finds expression in and through us (see v. 12). The Greek *meth' hēmōn* ("with us") suggests that we are active in the expression of love. Even though love is from God and is in reality God loving others through us, we are not mere passive channels through which His love flows. God indwelling us produces this love, but we also actively participate in the exercise of love.

And all of this is for a purpose: "that we may have boldness in the day of judgment" (concerning "boldness," see remarks on 3:21). One of the functions of love in the believer's life is the impartation of a bold confidence that will enable him to stand before the judgment seat of Christ without fear or shame.

The judgment referred to cannot be the judgment of the wicked, since only the wicked will appear there.

The assurance which love provides is based on the fact that "as he is, so are we in this world." The believer's confidence is based upon his likeness to Christ. Even before He comes and we become like Him (3:2), believers now are like Him in this world. And the similarity to which John refers is found in the fact that we love one another with the same kind of love that moved Him to lay down His life for us. Since we are like the One who is to be our Judge, we may face the judgment with perfect assurance.

Negative statement (4:18). By stating the same truth negatively, John proves and explains the statement in verse 17. The fear of which he speaks is not the reverence or respect which a person has for God or a son for his father. Such fear can and should coexist with love. On the contrary, this is dread or even terror which enslaves; it is the opposite of the bold confidence of verse 17. Where such fear exists there can be no love, and vice versa, for "perfect love casteth out fear." This is true because of what fear is and what love is. "Fear, the most self-centered of all emotions, can be analyzed as a heightened awareness of self occasioned by what are deemed to be threats to the self."[9] Love is quite the opposite. It is instead a diminishing of self-concern and a heightened awareness of others. Thus the two emotions vary inversely. The more fear there is, the less the love; the more one is occupied with love, the less he fears.

What John says in verse 18 is true of love and fear in general, as present-day psychology and psychiatry have shown. The apostle, however, uses the article before the two nouns, thus referring to a particular love and fear. The love is the selfless, Godlike love of the preceding context. It is the love that shows us to be like Christ (v. 17). Fear is the fear of the Judge and of the day of judgment (v. 17). Thus, love casts out fear because our love proves our likeness to Christ and gives confident assurance so that we need not fear to appear before Him at the judgment seat.

Although it is true that "fear hath torment," it should be noted that the Greek word *kolasin* really means punishment rather than torment. Fear, then, is not merely the dread of future punishment; it is itself punishment for the one who is possessed by it. Modern psychology recognizes fear as one of the most destructive of emotions.

The one who is habitually fearing (Greek present tense) "is not made perfect in love." In such a person love has not reached its goal of full expression in deed and in truth (3:18).

Statement of source (4:19). John now returns to the subject of love's source, and thus of the source of assurance. The best Greek manuscripts do not read "We love him" but simply "We love." The object of love is not in view in this verse; it is simply the fact that "we habitually love" (Greek present tense). The reason why we love is that God "first loved us." In this clause the verb "loved" is in the aorist tense, referring to a particular point in history. It is the same verb form as in verse 10, "he loved us," which speaks of the historical act of sending His Son to die for us.

The words of the apostle show strong contrast: *We,* on our part, love, because *He,* on His part, first loved us. His love enables us to love because, as a result of it, He who is love now indwells us. Also, we now love because He has become our Example, teaching us and persuading us to love. However we view it, love finds its origin in God; and because He is the Author of love, He is also the Author of assurance (v. 17).

THE NECESSITY OF BROTHER LOVE (4:20–5:5)

John now discusses the person who professes to love God but does not love his fellow Christian. Perhaps this was true of the Gnostics against whom the epistle was written. Such a distinction, declares the apostle, is impossible. Love for one's brother is demanded by love for God. The one cannot exist without the other.

Brother love demanded by logic (4:20). The hypothetical case which the author proposes is stated in the strongest terms: "If a man say, I *love* God, and *hateth* his brother, he is a *liar.*" This indicates that the claim is manifestly self-contradictory. Love for God and hatred for brother cannot possibly coexist in the same heart. Thus with typical Johannine brusqueness, the claim is dismissed as a lie.

John then proceeds to give reasons for his abrupt pronouncement. The first reason is simply the application of common sense (v. 20*b*). It is obviously easier to love someone whom we can see than someone whom we have never seen. A fellow Christian is visible and his needs are obvious. Therefore, we are easily able not only to feel love for him but to perform acts of love in his behalf. God is not visible, and it is thus much more difficult both to love Him and to manifest that love in action. If we do not fulfill the easier obligation, we certainly have not done that which is more difficult. Hence, if we claim that we love God, love of brother is demanded by simple logic.

Brother love demanded by divine commandment (4:21). Not only is it reasonable that love for God must be accompanied by love for one's brother, but it is His express command that such should be true. "This commandment have we from him." Since the preceding verse speaks of God, it is best to understand that He, not Christ, is the Giver of the commandment in verse 21. The substance of the commandment is "that he who loveth God love his brother also." Several rather involved explanations of this verse have been put forth by various commentators. The most obvious meaning, however, is that God has commanded that we love both God and our brother. He does not condone the love of one and not the other. Where do we find such a command? It seems most natural to see here a reference to Jesus' quotation of two Old Testament commands (Mt 22:37-39; Mk 12:29-31). The same God who said, "Thou shalt love the Lord thy God" (Deu 6:5), said also, "Thou shalt love thy neighbour" (Lev 19:18). If it be objected that, whereas the term *brother* is limited to a fellow

Christian the word *neighbor* refers to anyone, it should be pointed out that the term *neighbor* certainly includes the fellow Christian.

Brother love demanded by the nature of the family relationship (5:1). That one who loves God should also love his fellow Christian is a direct result of the new birth. At this point John again stresses the relationship of belief and love (cf. 4:14-16). This is another instance of the interweaving which characterizes the third cycle of the epistle. The test of belief in the incarnate Son does not stand alone, but is integrally related to the test of love. The latter is the natural result of the former.

To believe "that Jesus is the Christ" is the same as to believe that Jesus is the Son of God. John is not using the term "Christ" in the Hebraic sense of the promised Messiah. Instead he adjusts his use to that of the Gnostics who distinguished between the human Jesus and the divine Christ. They said that the Christ came upon Jesus át His baptism; John insists that Jesus and Christ are one and the same Person. And anyone who confesses the identity of the Two "is born of God."

The truth being stressed in 5:1 is the same as in 4:20, namely, love of God must be accompanied by love of one's Christian brother. Because of the family relationship and the common life which has been received through new birth, the children will not only love their Father ("him that begat"), but they will also love their brother ("him . . . that is begotten of him").

Brother love evidenced by love for God (5:2-5). Again, as elsewhere in 1 John, the phrase "by this" refers to what follows. Thus, John is saying that "we know that we love the children of God" by this, namely, that "we love God, and keep his commandments" (v. 2). This is the reverse of what we might have expected. The apostle does not say that we can know that we love God by the fact that we love God's children. Instead, it is love for God that proves we love God's people. The key to John's reasoning is found in the words "and keep his commandments" and in the explanation of verse 3 that "this is the love of God, that we keep his commandments." Thus, the apostle's reasoning goes something like this:

1. Love for God is the same thing as obeying His commandments (v. 3; cf. Jn 14:15, 21).
2. One of His two great commandments is the injunction to love one's neighbor as oneself (Lev 19:18).
3. Therefore, when we truly love God we know that we are loving our neighbors (and this includes God's children).

John is continuing to stress the idea set forth in 4:20. A person cannot love God without loving the children of God. The two loves are necessary companions; neither can exist without the other.

It is worth noting that, as in numerous previous references to love and obedience in 1 John, the verbs appear in the present tense ("love the children," v. 2; "love God," v. 2; "keep his commandments," vv. 2-3). John is talking about the habitual practice of love and obedience—not sporadic occurrences, but continuing action.

It is obvious that the "love of God" (v. 3) is love *for* God rather than love of which God is the Author. Our love for God is shown by our obedience to Him.

In verses 2-3 we see more of the practice of interweaving which is characteristic of 4:7—5:12. Not only are love for God and love for His people woven together, but love and obedience also are interwoven.

To these statements about love for God and for His children, John adds, almost parenthetically, "And his commandments are not grievous" (v. 3). The word "grievous" (*bareiai*) refers to a load that is excessively heavy. The noun form of the word (*barē*) occurs in Galatians 5:2, describing a load which is too weighty for one person to bear. But God's commandments are not too heavy for a person to bear. It is possible for us to keep them, not because the commandments are light, but because we are given the ability to fulfill their demands.

The apostle's added remark that the commandments are not burdensome requires an explanation, which follows in verses 4-5. Verse 4 begins with the word "for" (*hoti,* "because") indicating that this verse explains the preceding statement. The reason why God's commands are not unduly heavy is that God in the new birth gives power to overcome the world. In fact, this evil system which is opposed to God and righteousness is actually being overcome (Greek present tense) by God's children. This is the unqualified declaration of the apostle (5:4).

To this statement John adds, "And this is the victory that overcometh the world, even our faith." The verb "overcometh" here is in the aorist tense, depicting punctiliar action, whereas in the first part of this verse it is in the present tense, denoting continuing action. Apparently the continuing victory of the child of God (v. 4*a*) has its beginning at a specific point of victory (v. 4*b*), probably when a person first places faith in Christ as Saviour. When we turn in faith to Christ we gain initial victory over the world in that its hold on us is broken. As a result of this faith we are born again and given the power for continuing victory.

The question which is raised and answered in verse 5 is intended to explain more fully the faith mentioned in the previous statement. It is not faith in general nor merely faith in God which overcomes the world. The overcomer is the person who "believeth that Jesus is the Son of God." This statement was aimed at the false teachers who were troubling John's readers, for they refused to admit that Jesus was more than mere man. Cerinthus, the Gnostic, asserted that the divine element (the Christ) came upon the Man Jesus at baptism, but he would never agree that Jesus was the God-Man, God the Son in human flesh.

In our day as well as in John's, the experience of new birth, with the resulting ability to keep God's commandments and overcome the world, comes only to the person who places his faith in Jesus Christ as the incarnate Son of God. He who confesses a mere human Jesus can never experience new birth.

These two verses (4-5) contain more of John's characteristic interweaving of the ethical and the doctrinal tests of the genuineness of a person's salvation. God's commandments, one of which requires that we love our brothers, can be fulfilled (v. 3) because the new birth gives us the power to overcome (v. 4*a*). This power to overcome is also declared to be the result of faith (v. 4*b*), of believing that Jesus is the Son of God (v. 5). In verse 1 John has already shown that the new birth is related to believing that Jesus is the Christ. Thus, belief in the incarnation results in new birth, and new birth, in turn, gives one the ability to keep God's commandments, including the directive that we love one another. Love and righteousness, therefore, are inseparably related to belief. The ethical test of salvation is never to be divorced from the doctrinal test. Assurance cannot be based merely on the fact that we have professed faith in Jesus as God's Son. In addition to the profession of faith, our lives must reveal the ethical signs of salvation. There must be the habitual love for the members of God's family as well as the continuing practice of righteousness in order for a person to be sure that he is saved.

THE CHRISTOLOGICAL ASPECT (5:6-12)

The discussion of love (4:7—5:3) led inevitably to the concept of belief in Jesus as God's Son (5:4-5), for faith results in new birth and new birth results in love for God's family. Thus it is natural for John to turn now to the discussion of belief in Christ.

In this section he describes the solid foundation upon which faith rests. Faith is not gullibility; it is based upon trustworthy testimony. The author points out, first, the coincident witness of historical facts and the Holy Spirit (5:6-9), and second, the experiential witness of eternal life (5:10-12).

THE COINCIDENT WITNESS OF HISTORICAL FACTS AND THE HOLY SPIRIT (5:6-9)

The three witnesses (5:6). On superficial reading, verse 6 appears to be an enigma which resists interpretation. Numerous explanations have been suggested, only one of which is in harmony with the historical occasion for the epistle and with the immediate context of the verse.

The words "This is he" refer back to Jesus, the Son of God (v. 5). He is the One who "came by water and blood." In verses 1 and 5 John has been stressing the fact that Jesus is the Christ, the Son of God. This emphasis was aimed at refutation of the teaching of Cerinthus that the divine Christ came upon the human Jesus at His baptism and left Him just prior to His death. The key to the enigma of the water and blood is found in the Cerinthian doctrine. Water refers to the baptism of Jesus, and blood speaks of His death. The statement that "he . . . came" fittingly describes the experience of baptism by which Jesus entered upon His public ministry.

Cerinthus would probably have agreed that the Christ "came by water," inasmuch as he held that it was at His baptism in water that the Christ came upon Jesus. However, Cerinthian doctrine would not agree that the Christ was in any way connected with the shedding of blood. Therefore, John stresses that it was "not by water only, but by water and blood." The Greek text is even more specific: "not by *the* water only, but by *the* water and by *the* blood." The insertion of the definite articles, no doubt, serves to point out *the* water of His baptism and *the* blood of His death.

To the elements of water and blood, the apostle adds the testimony of the Holy Spirit: "It is the Spirit that beareth witness." According to John 15:26 a major activity of the Spirit is bearing witness concerning Christ. In this context He testifies concerning the fact that Jesus is the Son of God (v. 5). How this testimony is given is not explained. However, it may be significant that the Spirit descended upon Jesus as a dove on the occasion of His baptism. John records the statement of John the Baptist that it was by this means that he recognized Jesus as the Son of God (Jn 1:33-34). This explanation of the Spirit's testimony seems to harmonize best with the context.

It is clear that the Spirit is eminently qualified to testify "because the Spirit is truth." As such He does not bear false witness concerning the incarnation of God's Son.

Agreement is unanimous among Bible scholars that most of verse 7 and the first part of verse 8 did not appear in the original Greek manuscript which came from the pen of the apostle John. The words "in heaven, the Father, the Word, and the Holy Ghost; and these three are one. And there are three that bear witness in earth" are known to be a later insertion.[10] The text of verses 7-8 should read, "For there are three that bear record, the Spirit, and the water, and the blood; and these three agree in one."

The witness to the incarnation of God's Son is threefold. According to the civil law of the Old Testament, two or three witnesses were necessary to establish a charge (Deu 19:15). So the fact of the incarnation is supported by the testimony of the Holy Spirit, by the testimony of Christ's baptism and by the testimony. In verse 8, however, the water and blood are also said to be witnesses; only the Spirit is there described as giving testimony. In verse 8, however, the water and blood are also said to bear witness. The testimony of the baptism to the incarnation of God's Son may well have been the word that came from heaven, "This is my beloved Son, in whom I am well pleased" (Mt 3:17). The manner in which the death of Christ bears witness to the incarnation of God's Son is not as easy to discern. It may be that, as in the declaration from heaven (Mt 3:17) the stress is on Christ's deity, in the crucifixion the emphasis is on His humanity. Only a flesh-and-blood human being could be nailed to a cross and shed his blood. Thus Jesus Christ is shown to be both God and Man.

The agreement of the witnesses (5:6). The significance of these three witnesses is seen in that they "agree in one" (v. 8). Literally the text reads, "And the three are unto the one," that is, they are for the one purpose. Their goal is one. The Spirit and the water and the blood combine their testimony to declare that Jesus Christ is not a mere man upon whom the divine Christ rested temporarily, as Cerinthus taught, but is in very truth the God-Man.

The superior worth of the witness of God (5:9). John concludes this section dealing with the witness of the historical facts and the Holy Spirit (5:6-9) by pointing up the supreme value of such testimony (v. 9). The conditional clause "If we receive the witness of men" is not intended to cast doubt upon the reception of human testimony. This particular Greek construction may be paraphrased, "Since we receive." It is taken for granted that we do receive the testimony of men. The use of the verb "receive" in the present tense suggests that it is common practice to accept such testimony (cf. Deu 19:15). In comparison to the testimony of men, however, "the witness of God is greater," that is, it is weightier, more authoritative and more trustworthy. This is true because God Himself is greater. As the omniscient God He knows all things (1 Jn 3:20); as the God of truth (Ps 31:5; 100:5; 146:6) He cannot lie (Titus 1:2).

The implied conclusion of the conditional clause "If we receive the witness of men" is that we certainly should receive the witness of God because it is greater. And what is "the witness of God which he hath testified of his Son"? It is this—the threefold witness of the water, the blood and the Holy Spirit. These three separate witnesses are in reality one because they come from God and they concern His Son. No more competent witness could be found than that of a father for his son, and when the Father is God this is the most competent witness of all.

THE EXPERIENTIAL WITNESS OF ETERNAL LIFE (5:10-12)

The three witnesses of verse 6 were external witnesses, the voice of the Father at Christ's baptism, the descent of the Spirit as a dove, and the shedding of blood. Verses 10-12 speak of an internal witness which corroborates the external testimony. Here the believer "hath the witness in himself" (v. 10). It is not merely something about which he has heard or read; it is not even something which he himself has merely seen or heard; it is rather something which he has experienced and which he possesses in his own person.

The present tense "believeth" indicates that the author is not thinking of any passing confidence, but of a faith which is a continuing experience. Furthermore, it is not merely intellectual acceptance. This verse contains two similar but differing expressions: "believeth on the Son" and "believeth not God." To believe on a person is to place confidence in that person and to commit oneself to him. On the other hand, to believe a person may be nothing more than believing what he says. The former expression occurs nearly forty times in John's gospel[11] (cf. Jn 3:16; 9:35; 11:25). Thus, the person who "hath the witness in himself" is the one who has placed abiding faith in the person of the Son of God. He is trusting in Christ for his salvation, which is far more than merely believing something about Christ or even believing something which Christ has said.

In contrast, John goes on in verse 10b to speak of believing God, and in this case it is believing what God has said, namely, His testimony. To refuse to believe this is to make God a liar. As in 1:10, this expression means to make God out to be a liar or to call God a liar. And this is what a person actually does when he refuses to believe what God has said concerning His Son. The word translated "record" (*martyria*) is the term for witness or testimony (cf. vv. 9-10).

In verse 10 John does not explain what the witness is which the believer has in himself. It is not until we come to verse 11 that we discover what the author has in mind. He declares, "And this is the record" (Greek, "testimony"). The remainder of the verse states the substance of God's testimony within the believer. It is "that God hath given to us eternal life." In the Greek text the words for eternal life are placed in an emphatic position and may be literally translated "Eternal life God gave to us." This arrangement points up the fact that the actual testimony is eternal life itself.

To the threefold objective historical testimony of verse 6, John has added the subjective experiential testimony of eternal life. And this, like the former testimony, is God's witness concerning His Son. It is an added witness to the fact that Jesus is God's Son. In fact, eternal life and the Son are intimately related, for "this life is in his Son." Eternal life resides in the Son because He actually *is* the life (Jn 11:25; 14:6; 1 Jn 1:2).

It therefore stands to reason that to have the Son is to have life (v. 12). A person cannot have the latter without the former. The Greek text has the definite article before the word "life" in both occurrences in this verse, thus pointing back to the life described in verse 11 as eternal life which is "in his Son."

John's point in verses 10-12 is that the internal possession of eternal life is a witness of God concerning His Son. It is, in fact, God's testimony that Jesus is His Son. The apostle's reasoning seems to be that the person who has eternal life can know experientially that he has it. He knows this because God's Spirit "beareth witness with our spirit, that we are the children of God" (Ro 8:16). To put it another way, the believer knows that he has eternal life because he is experiencing fellowship with God. As Stott points out, "The experience of fellowship with God through Christ" is eternal life.[12] Furthermore, the Christian also knows that he entered this experience of life by trusting in Jesus Christ. Thus, the fact that receiving Christ brought eternal life is testimony that Jesus is in reality the Son of God.

The Gnostic Cerinthus and his followers denied that Jesus was the Christ, the Son of God. In response to this denial, John advances two kinds of testimony to support belief in divine sonship. The first is the objective historical testimony of water, blood and Holy Spirit (v. 6), which shows that Jesus was actually both God and Man. The second kind of testimony is the subjective witness of eternal life (vv. 10-12). The Gnostic could offer nothing but his empty speculations in proof of his assertions. The Christian can cite the voice from heaven (Mt

3:17), the descent of the Spirit as a dove (Mt 3:16), and the shedding of actual blood by a real human Jesus to prove that Jesus was both Man and God. In addition, he has the inner proof of eternal life received by trusting Christ as Saviour.

Conclusion: Great Certainties of the Christian Life (5:13-21)

With verse 12 of chapter 5, the final movement of John's argument comes to an end. The remainder of the epistle is given to concluding remarks. These, however, are not in the nature of casual, disconnected greetings or bits of personal information. Instead they comprise a compelling climax to all that has gone before. It has not been the apostle's aim to create uncertainty in the minds of believers, but rather to provide for them grounds for assurance. The same tests which served to identify those who were Gnostics, likewise served to reveal those who were genuine children of God. Thus, John concludes his epistle by "ringing the changes" on the subject of assurance. Over and over again he declares, "We know." Like a musical composer bringing his composition to an end with a grand crescendo, the author of 1 John rises to the highest point of the whole epistle in these concluding verses.

THE CERTAINTY OF ETERNAL LIFE (5:13)

Although verse 13 is rooted in the immediately preceding context, the expression "these things" must not be limited to the matters discussed there, for, as Lenski points out, what John wrote in those verses really involves all of the rest of the epistle.[13] Thus, as the author begins this concluding section, he is looking back on the book as a whole and explaining his aim in writing.

The purpose of the fourth gospel was that unbelievers might believe and thus receive life (Jn 20:30-31); the purpose of the first epistle is that those who do "believe on the name of the Son of God" may know that they "have eternal life." John has written that believers who are confronted with false teaching, such as Gnosticism, may have assurance and not be shaken by the error with which they are confronted. If one finds that he is walking in the light (1:7), confessing his sins (1:9), obeying Christ's commands (2:3-5), loving fellow believers (2:9-11; 3:14-17), believing in Jesus as God's incarnate Son (2:22-23; 4:1-6; 5:1, 5), and practicing righteousness (2:29; 3:6-10*a*), he can be assured by "these things" that he has eternal life. And because he possesses this assurance, he will not be shaken by any of the disturbing assertions of the vendors of error.

It should be noted that the best Greek manuscripts do not contain the words translated "and that ye may believe on the name of the Son of God."

THE CERTAINTY OF ANSWERED PRAYER (5:14-17)

THE CERTAINTY STATED (5:14-15)

The certainty of answered prayer is described as "the confidence that we have in him" (v. 14). The believer may possess the kind of bold confidence which produces freedom of speech in God's presence (*parrēsia*; see 2:28). Such confidence, however, is conditioned upon asking "according to his will." If we know that our request is in harmony with God's will, we may ask in full assurance that He listens favorably to our petition. This is not merely adding "if it be Thy will" to our prayers. It is knowing that we are asking for something which it is God's will to give.

The knowledge that what we ask for agrees with God's will can best be derived from God's Word. If our request is in accord with God's revealed will we may be sure of a favorable hearing. It is not enough to *feel* that it is in harmony with the divine will. Such subjective confidence may well be completely without foundation in fact. Nor can we force God to adjust to our will. Instead, we are to adjust our desires and petitions to His will.

The assurance that God has given our request a favorable

hearing assures us that "we have the petitions that we desired of him" (v. 15). The verb "have" is not future "we shall have"; it is present. "We have" at the present time that for which we have asked. Although in reality the answer to our prayer has not yet been realized, it is ours nevertheless. The answer may be days or months or years in coming, but God grants it to us immediately inasmuch as it is in harmony with His will.

The order of John's reasoning in these two verses (14-15) is as follows: (1) we ask in accordance with God's will; (2) we therefore know that God listens favorably to our request; and (3) thus we know that the request is granted to us. The basic assurance is that God grants requests for things which are in agreement with His will.

THE CERTAINTY ILLUSTRATED (5:16-17)

The subject of the sin unto death is introduced as an illustration of answered prayer. The Christian may pray with confidence for a fellow believer who is engaged in "sin which is not unto death" (v. 16). In light of the condition set down in verse 14, it appears that John is sure such a prayer is in accord with God's will, and thus God will hear and grant the request. On the other hand the "sin unto death" is not an object for confident intercession. John does not say we should pray concerning it, nor does he say we should not.

But what is the sin unto death? A number of interpretations have been advanced, none of which is completely without difficulty. Perhaps the most common view in conservative circles is that which sees the sin unto death as the sin of a Christian which results in physical death rather than spiritual death (cf. 1 Co 11:30). If so, we may ask why such sin is not the subject for confident prayer. The interpretation which is most probable is one which grows out of the context of this epistle. In 1 John there are two classes of sin. There is the sin which a believer may commit (2:1) and which he will confess (1:9), and there is the practice of sin which marks a man out as a child of Satan rather than God (3:8, 10). The latter is the practice of unrighteousness on the part of one who denies that Jesus is God's incarnate Son. This is the sin of the Gnostic whom John designates as an antichrist (2:18). There is no assurance that God will answer prayer for such a person, for he is a professed Christian who has committed himself to the adamant propagation of error and to unrestrained wickedness.

On the other hand "there is a sin not unto death" (v. 17). This may well be the act which a genuine Christian commits when he falls into sin, not because he adamantly rejects Jesus as God's incarnate Son, but simply because he is weak and not yet completely delivered from sin's depravity. Concerning a Christian who is involved in such a sin, we may pray with assurance that God will answer "and . . . give . . . life for them that sin not unto death" (v. 16).

THE CERTAINTY OF VICTORY (5:18)

A superficial reading of verse 18 presents several problems. (1) Is it true that the child of God does not sin at all? (2) Can he actually keep himself so that he will not sin? (3) Is he so safe that the devil cannot even touch him? Each of these ideas seems to be contradictory to other passages of Scripture.

In regard to the first problem, it has already been shown that the child of God does not habitually engage in sin (see comment on 3:9). He may commit individual acts of sin (2:1-2), but he does not live in sin. The same present tense verb is used in 5:18 as in 3:9, indicating that John is declaring that "no one who has been born of God habitually engages in sin."

This, however, is not because the child of God "keepeth himself," the second problem. Whereas the verb translated "is born" is the perfect tense stressing the results of the action, the verb "is begotten" appears in the aorist tense, pointing back to a historical occurrence. The reason for the change of tenses seems to be that the author is speaking of different persons. The perfect tense "is born" refers to the Christian, but the aorist tense "is begotten" speaks of Christ, the only begotten Son of God. The One who is keeping the child of God, then, is not the believer himself, but it is Christ. This is confirmed by the fact that the better Greek manuscripts have *auton* ("him") rather than *heauton* ("himself"). Thus, the inconsistency is removed. Scripture does not teach that the Christian can keep himself from sin. Christ alone can accomplish this.

Finally, the third problem, the word "toucheth" is not an adequate translation of *haptetai*. The Greek word literally means "to fasten oneself to" something or someone. Thus, John is assuring us that Satan cannot lay hold on the child of God. He may touch the believer, but he cannot take hold of him and keep him in his grip.

THE CERTAINTY OF TWO GREAT RELATIONSHIPS (5:19)

The assurance to which John refers in this verse concerns two family relationships. First, he speaks of the family of God—"we are of God." This is the same as the statement made in 4:6, and in reality it harks back to 3:9-10. The Greek prepositional phrase *ek tou theou* ("of God") speaks of the source from which the believer comes. It is the equivalent of saying (3:9) that he has been "born of God" (*gegennēmenos ek tou theou*). Upon the basis of the proofs set forth in this epistle we can know that we are members of God's family.

The second family relationship is not stated in parallel terms. Just as we know that we are *of* God, so we are sure that "the whole world" is *in* the devil's sphere. The term "world," being set in contrast to those who are "of God," must refer to the people of the world. This would include all who have not been born into the family of God. The word translated "wickedness" is the same term rendered "wicked one" in verse 18. Thus the unsaved people of the world dwell wholly within the sphere of Satan's dominion and, what is more, they lie there in evident helplessness.

THE CERTAINTY OF THE INCARNATION (5:20)

The final declaration of certainty reflects the occasion which called forth this epistle. Gnosticism denied that God's Son became incarnate. In contrast John asserts, "We know that the Son of God is come." The Gnostics claimed to possess special knowledge (*gnōsis*), but we have "an understanding" imparted to us by the Son of God, and we are enabled to know the true God. That the designation "him that is true" refers to the Father is indicated by the following reference to "his Son Jesus Christ." The knowledge which we have received is not speculative nor theoretical, for we "know *him,*" not merely *about* Him. The experiential nature of this knowledge is further emphasized by the fact that "we are in him." So close and vital is our fellowship that only such a mystical expression of intimate relationship can describe it.

John concludes this final declaration of Christian knowledge by reiterating his assertion that our God is "the true God," the genuine One in contrast to all false gods. In addition, He is "eternal life." Just as God is Spirit (Jn 4:24) and light (1 Jn 1:5), and love (1 Jn 4:8), so He is life. Not only is He the living God, but He *is* life itself, the source of it and the Giver of it.

CONCLUDING EXHORTATION (5:21)

John concludes the epistle with a fatherly reminder to his "little children" to keep themselves "from idols." Since they have intimate knowledge of the true God, any worship of dead idols is totally unreasonable. Since they were, for the most part, Gentile converts living in the idolatrous cities of Asia, this urgent command was no doubt most fitting.

2 JOHN

INTRODUCTION AND OUTLINE

DURING THE FIRST CENTURY the message of Christ was carried from town to town by traveling preachers and teachers. Because of the Roman roads, the Roman system of law, and the presence of Roman soldiers everywhere, it was safer to travel throughout the empire then than it ever had been before or would be again until modern times.

Not only did Christian leaders avail themselves of the opportunity to carry the truth to other lands, but the Gnostic teachers likewise took to the roads in order to propagate their error far and wide. Both Christians and Gnostics depended upon the hospitality of believers for their support while traveling. It was the custom to show Christian love by taking a traveling teacher into one's home and giving him provisions for the next leg of his journey.

John's second epistle was occasioned by the willing hospitality of a Christian lady, perhaps in the province of Asia. Although her name is not given, she and her family were well known to the apostle. Apparently, in the name of Christian love, she had taken Gnostic teachers into her home overnight, not realizing the significance of her act. In order to warn this hospitable Christian woman against the indiscriminate practice of love, John wrote this short note.

Although the name of the author does not appear in the text, the similarity to 1 John in style, vocabulary and content leaves no doubt but that the apostle John was the author. The fact that he calls himself an elder (v. 1) has caused some to question apostolic authorship. However, Peter likewise referred to himself by the same title (1 Pe 5:1), and there is no reason to deny that both men, in addition to being apostles, also served as local church officials.

The similarity of John's second epistle to his first one is most noticeable. Such terms and expressions as "love," "truth," "walking in truth," "commandment," "from the beginning," "deceivers," "antichrist" and "abide" are common to both epistles. The heresy confronting the elect lady seems to have been the same as that threatening the readers of 1 John (cf. 1 Jn 4:2-3 with 2 Jn 7). The date of writing is not known, but its evident relationship to the first epistle would seem to suggest that it was written during the same general period (A.D. 90-95).

I. INTRODUCTION (vv. 1-3)

    A. Author and recipients (vv. 1-2)
    B. Greeting (v. 3)

II. COMMENDATION (v. 4)

III. EXHORTATION AND WARNING (vv. 5-11)

    A. The believer exhorted (v. 5)
    B. Love explained (v. 6)
    C. The exhortation justified (v. 7)
    D. The believer warned (v. 8)
    E. The enemy and the believer contrasted (v. 9)
    F. The believer instructed (vv. 10-11)

IV. CONCLUSION (vv. 12-13)

COMMENTARY ON 2 JOHN

Introduction (vv. 1-3)

UNLIKE 1 JOHN, this second letter opens with the standard first century epistolary introduction. The Greek papyri reveal that it was customary for letters to begin with the names of the author and the recipient, followed by a greeting.

AUTHOR AND RECIPIENTS (vv. 1-2)

Instead of identifying himself by name, John refers to himself as "the elder." Although this term could refer to a person of advanced age, it is more likely that it is here employed to designate an officer in a local church. The word is used interchangeably with the term "bishop" in Titus 1:5, 7 and Acts 20:17, 28. In the second passage these officials are assigned the work of the shepherd or pastor. It was probably in the Ephesian church that John served as an elder.

The designation "elect lady" has been interpreted as referring either to a group or to an individual. Variations of the group view include (1) the whole church, (2) the church at Babylon, and (3) an unnamed local church. Individuals suggested include (1) the virgin Mary, (2) Martha, (3) a lady named Electa, (4) a Christian woman named Kyria, and (5) an anonymous influential woman in one of the Asian churches. Of all these views the two most commonly held are those of the unnamed local church and the anonymous woman of Asia.

Nothing in the passage demands that John be understood as writing to a local church. It is most unnatural that a simple

101

letter like 2 John should contain such an involved and sustained figure of speech. Not only would the lady represent a local church (v. 1), but her children would have to represent church members (vv. 1, 4) and her elect sister, another local congregation (v. 13). It is much more natural to take these expressions literally, in which case the elect lady would be a specific woman with grown children and a sister who was a Christian.

That the love which John professes is not romantic in nature is obvious for several reasons: (1) It is love for the woman and her children, as the plural pronoun "whom" indicates. (2) "All they that have known the truth" also love this woman and her family. (3) This love is closely associated with "the truth." The definite article—"They that have known *the* truth" (v. 1) and "for *the* truth's sake" (v. 2)—shows that John is speaking of Christian truth, the gospel.

The reason why John and other believers loved this family was "for the truth's sake" (v. 2) or "because of the truth" (RSV). Christian love is the product of truth dwelling in the believer. This does not mean merely that truth persuades us to love one another. As John explains in 1 John 5:1, the belief of the truth that "Jesus is the Christ" results in new birth, and new birth results in mutual love because we have become members of the family of God. Thus, fellowship among God's people is inseparable from the truth. We cannot sacrifice the fundamentals of the Christian faith without sacrificing the indispensable bond of all true fellowship, which is love.

The word "truth" occurs five times in the first four verses of this epistle, indicating the heavy emphasis that the author is placing on the matter. In the light of the remainder of the letter (especially vv. 7-11), it is apparent that John has stressed the truth in direct contrast to the error of the Gnostics, which constituted a dangerous threat to the elect lady. It is also to be noted that love and truth are inseparably tied together, thus preparing for the main lesson of the letter that truth must always govern the exercise of love.

GREETING (v. 3)

The usual greeting among the Hebrews was the term *shālôm* ("peace"; cf. Lk 10:5). The Greek greeting was *chairein*, which literally meant "to rejoice" (Ja 1:1). The latter occurred regularly in papyrus letters of the first three centuries. Christian writers, however, developed a distinctive form of greeting which, although it varied from person to person, was basically the same. The simplest form was "Grace and peace" (Ro 1:7; 1 Co 1:3; 1 Pe 1:2). In the pastoral epistles this greeting is expanded to "Grace, mercy, and peace" (1 Ti 1:2; 2 Ti 1:2; Titus 1:4), and it is this form that John employs in his second epistle.

A comparison with the pastorals, however, will show that John adds his own distinctive touch. The greeting comes from his pen, not as a wish or prayer, but as a declaration of assurance. In the Greek text the future tense of the verb "to be" appears, so that what John actually says is "There shall be with us grace, mercy, and peace." These benefits are assured for all of God's people. Just as the truth "shall be with us for ever" (v. 2), so, likewise, shall grace, mercy and peace. Plummer explains that grace is God's favor toward sinners; mercy is His compassion for the misery of sinners; and peace is "the result when the guilt and misery of sin are removed."[1]

As in most of the New Testament epistolary greetings, the author indicates that these blessings come "from God the Father, and from the Lord Jesus Christ." John, however, adds that Christ is "the Son of the Father," which is no doubt aimed at the Gnostic teachers who denied that Jesus is God's Son. The greeting concludes with the two terms around which the message of the epistle revolves. The blessings of grace, mercy and peace are ours in the sphere of "truth and love." These two elements are never separated from each other in God, nor should they be divorced from one another in His people.

Commendation (v. 4)

Before coming to the main subject of his letter, the apostle commends the family of the elect lady. He "rejoiced greatly" because he had found some of her children "walking in truth." Such a statement of commendation, appreciation or thanksgiving is common in the letters of the New Testament (cf. Ro 1:8; 1 Co 1:4-8; Phil 1:3-8). John does not say where he had found these children walking in truth, but it was no doubt in some of his travels among the churches. The words "of thy children" do not necessarily indicate that not all of the woman's children were so walking. John may be saying no more than that he had come across some of the children, but he had not met all of them.

The expression "walking in truth" is most significant, for it is a corrective against two evils. First, it denies that a life acceptable to God can be lived apart from truth. Truth is the foundation for living. Second, it denies that truth should be held theoretically. Truth is not merely to be believed; it is to be lived. These children of the elect lady were conducting their lives in the sphere of and in accordance with the truth of God.

Exhortation and Warning (vv. 5-11)
THE BELIEVER EXHORTED (v. 5)

John now begins to move in the direction of the problem which called forth this letter, namely, the indiscriminate exercise of love. However, lest the elect lady misunderstand and think that he is deprecating love, he exhorts her to love her fellow Christians. He does not command, although as apostle and elder he could have done so. Instead he requests, and the term which he uses (*erōtō*) describes the plea as a request made of an equal. John, the apostle, places this Christian woman on an equal plane with himself.

The commandment which forms the basis for the author's plea is not "a new commandment," but it is one which they had possessed from the beginning of their Christian experience.

Here, as in the parallel passage of 1 John 2:7, stress is placed on the continued possession of the commandment from the beginning until now. The commandment is, therefore, not new. However, notice that in 1 John 2:8 this old command- ment is also called new, no doubt because Jesus Himself re- ferred to it as a new commandment. The substance of this divine command is "that we love one another" not momen- tarily but habitually (Greek present tense).

LOVE EXPLAINED (v. 6)

The Bible does not view love as mere sentiment nor empty profession. Thus John explains that the love of which he speaks in verse 5 consists of walking "after his commandments" (v. 6). Love that is genuine reveals itself in obedience. This reminds one of Paul's dictum "Love is the fulfilling of the law" (Ro 13:10). If we love one another, we will treat one another in accordance with God's commands. We will not steal from one another; we will not deceive one another; we will not kill one another. Such action, however, will not be motivated by law, but by love.

In the second part of verse 6, John changes from the broader first person plural "we" to the more specific second person plural "ye." He now makes his application directly to the elect lady and her children. Also, he moves from the plural "commandments" to the singular "commandment." The com- mandments are the precepts of the law; the commandment is the injunction to love (cf. v. 5). Thus, the author in reality is reasoning in a circle. However, this kind of circular reasoning does not militate against the validity of his logic. In verse 5 obedience to the commandment of the Lord produces love; in verse 6a love produces obedience to the commands; again in verse 6b obedience to Christ's command produces love. And love is an attitude which affects life, for we are to "walk in it." This somewhat involved train of thought shows how closely interwoven are the concepts of love, on the one hand, and obedience and action on the other.

THE EXHORTATION JUSTIFIED (v. 7)

Having assured the elect lady that believers are commanded of the Lord to love one another, John now proceeds to the main subject of his letter. What should be the attitude of the Christian toward the "many deceivers" who "are entered into the world" (v. 7)? In the name of love, should he treat them with Christian hospitality?

Verse 7 begins with the conjunction "for," indicating that the following statement is the reason for heeding the exhortation of verses 5-6. Believers are to cultivate genuine love for one another because "many deceivers are entered into the world" (v. 7). As in 1 John 4:1, John is referring to the fact that many false teachers are traveling from place to place propagating their error. These are individuals who "confess not that Jesus Christ is come in the flesh." This is the same as saying that these deceivers are denying the truth of the incarnation (cf. 1 Jn 2:22). The heresy of which 2 John speaks is the identical Gnostic error refuted in 1 John 4:2-3. False teachers such as Cerinthus refused to believe that the divine Christ actually came in human flesh.

That John is not speaking of the second coming of Christ is evident for several reasons. (1) We know of no first century heresy which denied a second coming in flesh. (2) The Gnostics did deny that the first coming was a coming in flesh. (3) The perfect tense "is come" in the parallel passage (1 Jn 4:2) points back to the first advent. (4) Flesh is more normally used of the mortal human body than of the immortal resurrection body.

John characterizes those who reject the incarnation of Christ as "the deceiver and the antichrist" (Greek text). According to Brooke, by this John means to lump together all of the Gnostics and describe them as *the* deceiver and *the* Antichrist *par excellence*. This is to say that the Gnostic heresy is the product of the archenemy of God and His people. It comes from Satan himself and is propagated by the spirit of Antichrist which is even now abroad in the world (1 Jn 4:3).

THE BELIEVER WARNED (v. 8)

The presence of many deceivers in the world is cause for the warning "Look to yourselves" or, in modern terms, "Watch yourselves." The present tense calls for continued vigilance, for the danger is ever present that heretical teachers may rob believers of the spiritual gains which have been made. The better Greek texts support the translation "that you lose not those things which we have wrought, but that you receive a full reward." It appears that John views the spiritual gains made in the lives of the elect lady and her family as produced by the labors of the apostle and his associates. The concept of a full reward may be that of a full day's pay, since the primary meaning of *misthos* is wages or pay. John is concerned that the elect lady not allow false teachers to so influence her that, when she stands before Christ's judgment seat, she will not receive the full reward which she might have had.

THE ENEMY AND THE BELIEVER CONTRASTED (v. 9)

John contrasts the one who goes beyond and the one who remains "in the doctrine of Christ" in verse 9. This doctrine is not teaching which comes from Christ; instead it is the teaching concerning Christ's incarnation which John has already pointed out in verse 7. The false teachers do not remain in the doctrine; that is, they do not continue to hold it. The Authorized Version's translation "Whosoever transgresseth" misses the point of contrast. The word translated "transgresseth" literally means "to go beyond or before." The Gnostics claimed to be advancing beyond the inferior concept of the incarnation. They assumed themselves to be progressive in their thinking as has so often been the case when doctrinal error has arisen in the church. Plummer wisely warns, "There is an advance which involves desertion of first principles; and such an advance is not progress but apostasy."[2] The one making such advance, declares John, "hath not God." No matter how profoundly he may discourse about knowing God, if he denies the incarnation,

he does not have Him. Christ declared, "No man cometh unto
the Father, but by me" (Jn 14:6).

In direct contrast John describes the person who "abideth
in the doctrine." (The words "of Christ" do not appear in the
best Greek manuscripts.) The one who remains in the sphere
of the truth "hath both the Father and the Son." The possession of eternal life cannot be divorced from the possession
of correct doctrine. When the truth is possessed meaningfully
and trustingly, the result is that God the Father and God the
Son become our God and our Saviour.

The Believer Instructed (vv. 10-11)

Verses 10-11 reveal the situation which led to the writing of
the letter. The conditional clause "If there come any unto
you, and bring not this doctrine" (v. 10) is a Greek simple
condition which assumes the reality of the situation described.
Persons who denied the doctrine of the incarnation had been
coming to the home of the elect lady. The prohibitions "Receive him not . . . neither bid him God speed" literally mean
"Stop receiving" and "Stop bidding." Apparently she had actually received such teachers into her house because she felt
that Christian love demanded that she show them hospitality.
John, however, insists that she stop this indiscriminate practice
of love.

In the early church numerous traveling teachers moved from
town to town, depending upon the hospitality of the Christian
people in each place. This is implied in John's commendation
of Gaius in 3 John 5-8. Gaius had shown Christian love in receiving traveling brethren under his roof and sending them
forth with provisions for their journey. The same practice is
urged upon Titus in Titus 3:13. In a day when there were no
missionary organizations for channeling missionary giving, the
simple exercise of Christian hospitality toward traveling teachers and evangelists was a primitive form of missionary support.
John is, therefore, forbidding the support of those whose teaching denies that Jesus is the incarnate Son of God.

To bid a person Godspeed suggests that we express the desire that God may bless his mission. The Greek term is the normal greeting *chairein,* which literally means "to rejoice." This suggests that the speaker wishes the traveler joy on his journey. Thus the translation "bid him God speed" is not far from the intention behind the greeting which John forbids.

Since such a strict prohibition may seem to be unjustified, the apostle proceeds in verse 11 to explain the reason for it. Although the explanation only mentions the greeting, it may be assumed that the act of hospitality is also included. The reason for not showing such hospitality to false teachers nor wishing them a prosperous journey is that by so doing the Christian becomes a "partaker of his evil deeds." The word *koinōnei* means "to share." When the elect lady provided lodging for the heretical teacher she was actually sharing in his work, for she was investing her own time and money in the propagation of his teaching.

The principle set forth in this verse is no less true today. Money represents that portion of life which was used in earning it. Therefore, the Christian actually invests a portion of his life in the cause to which he donates his funds. The Christian's money should be given only to such persons as are proclaiming the incarnate Christ, God's Son who came in human flesh to be our Saviour.

Conclusion (vv. 12-13)

The nature of the concluding remarks in verses 12-13 seems to confirm the view that the elect lady was an individual rather than a church. This is further indicated by the close similarity to the conclusion of 3 John, a letter which all agree was written to a single person.

It is further apparent that John is well acquainted with this Christian woman and her family for he has "many things to write" (v. 12) to them. However, he has written only that which is most urgent. The other things will be kept until he can speak with them "face to face." There may be two reasons for waiting until he comes to complete his communication to this family. First, writing materials were far from plentiful in the first century and, second, the spoken word is much more effective and understandable than the written. He wants to speak to these friends "face to face" (literally "mouth to mouth"; cf. Num 12:8) . His purpose was "that our joy may be full." The Greek construction stresses the continuing state of fullness which John intends. The face-to-face fellowship which he confidently awaits will contribute to the continuing joy of all concerned, for such personal fellowship is one of God's means of increasing and preserving genuine Christian joy. Although joy is the fruit of the Holy Spirit (Gal 5:22) , it is not fostered in isolation, but in the give and take of interpersonal relationships with other believers.

The final words concerning "the children of thy elect sister" have been variously interpreted. Some have argued that these are the members of the church of Ephesus, since John no doubt wrote from that city. This view assumes that the designation "elect lady" is used figuratively of a local church somewhere in the province of Asia. Others have argued that the term "elect sister" is to be understood literally of an individual Christian woman, as is the "elect lady" (v. 1). Robertson suggests that the "elect sister" was deceased, since only her children are mentioned. Conner thinks John may have been a guest in the house of the "elect sister" when he wrote. The last two views are obviously mere guesses. It is clear, however, from the singular pronouns "thy" and "thee" that the elect lady is an individual rather than a church. All other attempts to explain these singular forms are labored and artificial. If the two ladies are interpreted as being individuals, it would be best to assume that the children of the sister were living in the city of Ephesus and that John had frequent contact with them. It may have been these children who informed John of the situation which gave rise to this letter.

3 JOHN

INTRODUCTION AND OUTLINE

THE SHORT LETTER of 3 John provides a glimpse of first century church life. Here reflected, on the one hand, is the practice of Christian hospitality toward traveling teachers and missionaries and, on the other hand, the perversion of spiritual leadership by a would-be church dictator.

Like 2 John, the third epistle is addressed to an individual, but, whereas the recipient of the second letter is left anonymous, the addressee of 3 John is explicitly named. Although the New Testament mentions three different persons who bore the name of Gaius (Ac 19:29; Ro 16:23; 1 Co 1:14), we cannot be sure whether any one of these individuals was the man to whom 3 John was sent. The name Gaius was as common in the first century Roman world as the names John or James are today.

That the epistle came from the same pen as 1 and 2 John is evident from the inescapable similarity in style and vocabulary. As examples consider the following agreements in vocabulary:

Elder (2 Jn 1; 3 Jn 1)
Love (1 Jn 2:10; 3:1, 10-11, 14-18; 4:7—5:3; 2 Jn 1, 5-6; 3 Jn 1, 6)
Truth (1 Jn 1:6, 8; 2:4, 21, 27; 4:6; 2 Jn 1-4; 3 Jn 1, 3-4, 8, 12)
Joy (1 Jn 1:4; 2 Jn 12; 3 Jn 4)
Walking in truth (2 Jn 4; 3 Jn 3-4)

In addition, the contrast of good and evil as spiritual tests (v. 11) reminds one of 1 John; and 3 John 13-14 is almost an exact duplicate of 2 John 12.

Such similarities, as well as a measure of likeness in subject matter, would seem to suggest that all three epistles were written about the same time (A.D. 90-95) .

The background for both 2 and 3 John is to be found in the practice of Christian teachers and missionaries traveling from community to community and from church to church. When such individuals came it was the custom for Christians to take them into their homes and provide them with lodging and provision for their ensuing journey.

It appears that such traveling teachers had come from John in Ephesus to the church of which Gaius was a member. He had received them with Christian hospitality, but Diotrephes, a local church leader, refused to receive them and sought to cast out from the fellowship those Christians who did. John's purpose in penning this letter to Gaius was to commend Gaius for his manifestation of Christian love and to assure him that Diotrephes would be dealt with in due time.

A comparison with 2 John reveals that these two letters are complementary to each other. Whereas 2 John warns against showing hospitality to false teachers, 3 John warns against refusing to show hospitality to those who proclaim the truth.

I. Introduction (vv. 1-2)
    A. Author and recipient (v. 1)
    B. Prayer (v. 2)

II. Commendation (vv. 3-8)
    A. Christian conduct in general (vv. 3-4)
    B. Christian hospitality in particular (vv. 5-8)

III. Condemnation (vv. 9-10)

IV. Exhortation (v. 11)

V. Recommendation (v. 12)

VI. Conclusion (vv. 13-14)

COMMENTARY ON 3 JOHN

Introduction (vv. 1-2)

THIS EPISTLE begins with a standard epistolary introduction which is very similar to that found in 2 John. In place of the greeting (2 Jn 3), however, the author here inserts a prayer for his reader (3 Jn 2). Both types of introduction were common in letters of John's time.

AUTHOR AND RECIPIENT (v. 1)

As in the previous letter, John refers to himself as "the elder," no doubt referring to an office which he held in the church at Ephesus (see remarks on 2 Jn 1). The recipient is described as "the wellbeloved Gaius," a designation which suggests that he was the kind of person whom people loved. The characteristics which called forth such esteem are illustrated in verses 5-8. However, not only do believers in general love Gaius, but John declares his own personal attitude, describing him as one "whom I love in the truth." The author makes the same assertion concerning the elect lady in 2 John (see remarks on 2 Jn 1).

PRAYER (v. 2)

The fact that Gaius is the kind of a man whom people love is further stressed in the term "Beloved," a designation which John repeats in verses 5 and 11. It may be debatable whether the desire which the author expresses in this verse is a prayer or merely a wish. The word *euchomai* may refer to either.

Numerous modern versions translate the word "I pray" (RSV, NEB, NASB, Williams, Beck, Montgomery, TEV). It should also be noted that this is a common term in papyrus letters, often with an obvious religious meaning. ("I pray to God that you are prosperous"; "I pray for your prosperity daily before all the gods"; "I pray to God that my letter finds you well.") [1] Thus, John is following the standard pattern for introducing a letter, expressing his desire for the recipient in the form of a prayer.

This is a rather remarkable prayer in that it reverses the terms of the comparison from the order which might have been expected. John prays that Gaius may prosper and be in health even as his soul prospers. Uppermost in the author's mind, apparently, were material prosperity and physical health. It might seem more natural to pray that a person may prosper spiritually as he is prospering in his business. However, that John could pray that Gaius may prosper materially as he is prospering spiritually is a high compliment to the level of spirituality which this beloved brother enjoyed.

Commendation (vv. 3-8)

Verses 3-8 explain what the author had in mind when he spoke of the spiritual prosperity of Gaius (v. 2). He refers first to Gaius' general Christian conduct (vv. 3-4) and then more specifically to his Christian hospitality (vv. 5-8).

CHRISTIAN CONDUCT IN GENERAL (vv. 3-4)

John knew that Gaius was prospering spiritually because "brethren came and testified" concerning the matter. This is a reference to traveling Christians who came to Ephesus and told the church about Gaius. There is no clear indication as to the identity of these visiting brethren. They may have been itinerant teachers or emissaries whom John had sent to the church with which Gaius and Diotrephes were connected (cf. v. 10). Whoever they were, they caused the apostle to rejoice by testifying concerning Gaius' truth ("the truth that is in thee"). This is not referring merely to truth which Gaius believed, but to truth which he practiced, as is evident from the following clause: "even as thou walkest in the truth." In John's writings, truth and righteousness, believing and living, are never separated. Belief of the truth is always accompanied by living in accordance with the truth. The present tense verb "walkest" indicates that Gaius was habitually practicing the truth which he possessed. Thus the apostle "rejoiced greatly" because of the Christian conduct of this beloved brother.

Having spoken in verse 3 of a specific instance of rejoicing concerning the conduct of Gaius, John advances to a more general statement of joy in verse 4. Here he lays stress on the extent of his joy. "I have no greater joy." Nothing exceeds John's interest in and concern for the spiritual welfare of his children. The Greek text, literally translated, says, "I do not have greater joy than these" (plural). Probably the plural demonstrative pronoun refers to numerous occasions of rejoicing when John heard that some of his children were walking in the truth. No doubt reports came to the aged apostle from time to time as traveling Christians visited Ephesus with news from the various churches of the province of Asia. The persons whom he designates as "my children" were in some sense his *own* children as the Greek possessive pronoun *ema* indicates. It would, therefore, seem most probable that these persons were his converts to Christ, although the term could refer to all who were under John's spiritual care, whether or not he was instrumental in their conversion.

It is noteworthy that the apostle rejoices not merely in the acceptance of the truth but in the continuing expression of that truth in life. The professed believer whose life shows no outward evidence of indwelling truth, far from being a cause for rejoicing, is instead reason for sadness. Truth believed but not expressed in life is truth which in reality is not believed at all. Truth genuinely believed will, without exception, find expression in the believer's life.

CHRISTIAN HOSPITALITY IN PARTICULAR (vv. 5-8)

The author now becomes more specific in his commendation of Gaius. He especially appreciates the manifestation of Christian hospitality which this beloved brother has shown. The words "thou doest faithfully" may be literally translated "you are doing a faithful thing" (v. 5). The activity of Gaius was a work which sprang from his Christian faith. The New Testament makes it clear that genuine faith is a faith which produces good works (cf. Eph 2:8-10; Ja 2:14-26). In the case of Gaius, his faith was expressing itself in hospitality. John refers to this activity as "whatsoever thou doest to the brethren." Apparently these persons were traveling Christians, perhaps teachers and evangelists, who had come to the town where Gaius lived.

The Authorized Version's translation "and to strangers" suggests a separate group of individuals other than the brethren. The better manuscripts, however, read *kai touto xenous* ("and this [to] strangers"). The brethren who came to Gaius were not known to him, but he was willing nevertheless to take them into his house and give them food and lodging. It is one thing to be hospitable to those whom we know, but to receive persons who are total strangers requires an even higher quality of hospitality.

John has heard about the faithful work of Gaius from the beneficiaries of his kindness. Apparently they have come to Ephesus and "have borne witness" concerning his love "before the church" (v. 6). By using the term "charity" ("love") the apostle calls attention to the real source of Gaius' action. He did not show hospitality out of neccessity nor for remuneration, but because of love. As everywhere in John's epistles, the author uses the term *agapē*, which speaks of an intelligent, deliberate, outgoing, self-giving love patterned after the love of God Himself. And it was a love for brethren whom he did not know personally but who were the objects of his love because they were brothers in Christ. This bears out the early description of Christians as people who loved one another before they knew each other. The real basis of such love is not the personality characteristics of the person being loved; instead it is that he is a brother in Christ, born of the same heavenly Father and sharing faith in the same Saviour.

The expression "whom . . . thou shalt do well" (v. 6*b*) was a common idiom in papyrus letters equal to our *please*.[2] Charles B. Williams translates it, "You will please send them off on their journey." John was requesting Gaius to continue the good work of faith for which he had become known. Here, however, we may gain further insight into the nature of this work. He is urged to "bring [them] forward on their journey," indicating not merely that he was to accompany them for a short distance, but that he was to give them provisions for the next stage of their trip. Such provision was not to be a mere token gift, but one worthy of God Himself ("after a godly sort"). As God freely and fully meets our needs, so Gaius was asked to provide for the immediate needs of the itinerant Christian workers who came his way.

The reason why these traveling brethren should be provided for is twofold (v. 7). First, "for his name's sake they went forth"; second, they received no help from "the Gentiles." John is not talking about contributing to any traveling Christian who comes along. Instead, he has in mind those who are engaged in Christian work, whether as teachers or as missionaries. Thus, Gaius' contribution was not to individuals as such, but to the work of the Lord in which these individuals were engaged.

The second reason for providing for their journey was that they were "taking nothing of the Gentiles." We are not here to understand the term "Gentile" literally, as referring to all non-Jews, but rather as a general term for pagans or heathen. These Christian workers were not receiving support from the unbelievers to whom they were taking the gospel message. This is not a complaint on John's part, for the biblical principle is that God's people, not unbelievers, should support God's work.

Since Christians cannot, nor should not, expect support from unbelievers, John concludes, "We therefore ought to receive such" (v. 8). The word "receive" literally means "to receive under." In this passage it is a term for hospitality, for receiving someone under one's roof and providing food and lodging. This Gaius had been doing (vv. 5-6*a*), and John urges him to continue the good work (vv. 6*b*-8). The apostle is speaking of the earliest method of missionary support, long before there were any organizations through which to channel such aid. By this simple practice of providing food and overnight accommodations as well as provisions for their coming journey, Gaius was helping to underwrite the work of these early missionaries of the gospel.

We ought to provide support for those who proclaim the gospel message in order "that we might be fellow-helpers to the truth" (v. 8). Just as the elect lady participated in the spread of error by giving to false teachers (2 Jn 11), so Gaius participated in the dissemination of the truth by contributing to those who proclaimed it.

Although the methods of missionary support are much more complex in the twentieth century, the same principle which John enunciated for the elect lady and for Gaius is no less applicable. Christian people must make sure that the missionaries to whom they give are proclaiming the truth, for by contributing to them they become participants along with them in their work.

Condemnation (vv. 9-10)

Whereas Gaius by his reception of itinerant teachers had given John reason for rejoicing, there was another member of the same local church, named Diotrephes, who was creating trouble by refusing to receive such teachers. In fact, he even refused to receive any written communication sent from John to the church (v. 9). Apparently he was in a position of leadership so that he could intercept such a letter and keep it from being read to the congregation. What the subject of the letter was which the apostle "wrote unto the church," we have no way of knowing for sure. It appears that it may have had to do with the coming of the traveling teachers or missionaries mentioned in the preceding verses (5-8) and again referred to in verse 10. It may be that John had sent a letter commending the traveling brethren to the church. Some have suggested that this letter to the church was 2 John, in which case the term "elect lady" would be a figurative reference to the church as a whole. There is no good reason, however, for understanding the term as being anything but literal.

The author points out the real cause of the trouble when he characterizes Diotrephes as one "who loveth to have the preeminence among them." Whether his was an elected position or a self-assumed one, we do not know. What is clear is that he was unwilling to share the prestige of leadership with anyone else, even with the apostle John. The desire for power and glory had become an obsession with him. Since that time, far too many others have followed in his inglorious footsteps, bringing shame to themselves and disgrace to the cause of Christ.

In verse 10 John assures Gaius that he will deal with the situation when he comes to visit the church. As verse 14 indicates, the apostle hopes to see Gaius soon. The expression "I will remember his deeds" means more than "I will not forget." It is the apostle's assurance that he will bring up the subject of Diotrephes' conduct. The present tense verbs "doeth," "prating," "receive," "forbiddeth" and "casteth" all indicate that these were habitual practices of Diotrephes. According to the author, this church dictator was guilty on four counts. First, he was "prating against us [John] with malicious words." The term "prating" means "to talk nonsense." Not only was Diotrephes' campaign against John characterized by nonsensical charges, but it was also expressed in "malicious words." The Greek term translated "malicious" refers to that which is wicked, evil or even vicious. It is used in a number of passages to describe the devil.

In the second place, Diotrephes was refusing to "receive the brethren" who came from John. He closed the door of his home to those traveling missionaries.

In the third place he forbade "them that would" receive them. Although the English word *forbid* refers to a spoken or written prohibition, the Greek word which it represents is much broader, depicting any kind of hindrance which may be placed in a person's way. Apparently Diotrephes was using any means available to hinder other church members from showing hospitality to the missionaries.

The fourth charge against this unscrupulous church dictator was that he was casting those "out of the church" who dared to show hospitality to the rejected brethren. So complete was Diotrephes' control of the church that he had actually taken to himself the power of excommunication. Whether or not Gaius was among those who had been put out is not indicated.

Exhortation (v. 11)

Having dealt with the unpleasant situation of dictatorial church leadership, John now exhorts Gaius not to be influenced by the bad example of Diotrephes. "Follow not that which is evil." The Greek is literally "Stop imitating." Although this construction normally represents the prohibition of an action already in progress, such an interpretation may be too harsh here. However, John at least seems to be reflecting a tendency on Gaius' part to be influenced by Diotrephes' evil ways, and the apostle would put a stop to such proneness. Instead Gaius is exhorted to be imitating "that which is good."

This prohibition and exhortation are supported by a basic principle which John states in typical antithetical form. Put positively, it is "He that doeth good is of God." The present tense verb speaks of a continuing practice of the good. As in 1 John (2:29; 3:9-10), such habitual conduct demonstrates that a person is "of God," that is, he has been born of God. Put negatively, John's principle is "He that doeth evil hath not seen God." Again it is the practice of evil which is in view (cf. 1 John 3:6, 8). To see God does not refer to seeing a physical form, for "God is a Spirit" (Jn 4:24) and "no man hath seen God at any time" (Jn 1:18). Instead, seeing Him is viewing Him with the eye of faith as Saviour and Lord.

Recommendation (v. 12)

Although there is no available information concerning the identity of Demetrius, it has often been supposed that he was the bearer of the letter to Gaius. Dana imagines that he carried the letter previously sent to the church and rejected by Diotrephes (v. 9). That some such contact with Gaius and the church had occurred seems evident from the wholehearted recommendation which John gives. All who know Demetrius have testified favorably concerning him. Even the truth bears witness, which no doubt means that since his life is in accord with the truth, the truth testifies concerning the kind of man he is. To those testimonies John adds his own witness because he knows that Gaius will not doubt his word.

Conclusion (vv. 13-14)

Concerning verses 13-14, see the comments on 2 John 12. There is a slight difference in vocabulary and grammatical structure between the two conclusions, but the content is basically the same. John "had many things to write," but he had decided not to communicate these matters "with ink and pen" (v. 13). In the second epistle, he speaks of "paper and ink" (2 Jn 12). The word translated "pen" is *kalamou*, meaning "reed," which was a common writing instrument in ancient times. John's reason for not penning a more lengthy letter may have been (1) the cost of writing materials, (2) the labor of writing with the crude instruments available, or (3) the personal nature of the matters to be discussed.

The better alternative would be to discuss these matters "face to face" (v. 14), and this John looked forward to doing. He hoped ("trust") to see Gaius shortly, by which he apparently

meant that he intended to come to Gaius' town to see him and
to deal with Diotrephes (v. 10).

The concluding greeting "Peace be to thee" is the typical
Hebrew saying which had been adopted by Christians as well
and which functioned both as a salutation and a farewell.
Christ Himself had used it when He greeted His disciples after
the resurrection (Jn 20:19, 21, 26). In view of the disturbing
situation created by Diotrephes, such a wish on John's part
would be particularly meaningful to Gaius.

In conclusion the apostle sends greetings from the friends
of Gaius who are in Ephesus, which may indicate that Gaius
lived in one of the towns of the province of Asia, not far from
Ephesus. The designation of Christians as "friends" rather
than "brethren" is unique in John's letters, although Jesus
used the term when speaking of those for whom He was about
to lay down His life (Jn 15:13).

John, in turn, asks that greetings be conveyed to persons who
are members of the same church as Gaius. The request that he
greet them "by name" indicates that the author does not want
them greeted as a group as in a congregation, but individually,
one by one, showing the personal affection which he had for
each of them.

FOOTNOTES

1 John

1. Irenaeus, *Against Heresies*, III. 11. 1.
2. R. C. H. Lenski, *The Interpretation of the Epistles of St. Peter, St. John and St. Jude*, p. 367.
3. Robert Law, *The Tests of Life, A Study of the First Epistle of John*, p. 21.
4. George G. Findlay, *Fellowship in the Life Eternal*, p. 199.
5. John R. W. Stott, *The Epistles of John*, p. 105.
6. A. T. Robertson, *Word Pictures in the New Testament*, 6:226.
7. Lenski, p. 479.
8. Law, p. 85.
9. Paul Hoon, "The First, Second, and Third Epistles of John," G. A. Buttrick, ed., *The Interpreter's Bible*, 12:286.
10. Bruce M. Metzger, *The Text of the New Testament*, pp. 101-2.
11. A. Plummer, *The Epistles of S. John*, J. J. S. Perowne, ed., *Cambridge Greek Testament for Schools and Colleges*, p. 117.
12. Stott, p. 183.
13. Lenski, p. 531.

2 John

1. A. Plummer, *The Epistles of S. John*, J. J. S. Perowne, ed., *Cambridge Greek Testament for Schools and Colleges*, pp. 133-34.
2. *Ibid.*, p. 138.

3 John

1. A. S. Hunt and C. C. Edgar, *Select Papyri*, Loeb Classical Library, 1:367, 369, 389.
2. Archibald T. Robertson, *Word Pictures in the New Testament*, 6:261; A. E. Brooke, *A Critical and Exegetical Commentary on the Johannine Epistles*, pp. 184-85.

BIBLIOGRAPHY

Alexander, William. *The Epistles of St. John. The Expositor's Bible.* W. Robertson Nicoll, ed. London: Hodder & Stoughton, 1889.

Alford, Henry. *The Greek Testament.* Vol. 4. Chicago: Moody, 1958.

Blaiklock, E. M. *Faith Is the Victory, Studies in the First Epistle of John.* Grand Rapids: Eerdmans, 1959.

Brooke, A. E. *A Critical and Exegetical Commentary on the Johannine Epistles. The International Critical Commentary.* S. R. Driver et al., eds. Edinburgh: T. & T. Clark, 1912.

Candlish, Robert S. *The First Epistle of John.* Grand Rapids: Zondervan, n.d.

Conner, Walter T. *The Epistles of John.* 2d ed., rev. Nashville: Broadman, 1957.

Dana, H. E. *The Epistles and Apocalypse of John.* Kansas City: Central Sem., 1947.

Findlay, George G. *Fellowship in the Life Eternal.* London: Hodder & Stoughton, n.d.

Hoon, Paul. "The First, Second, and Third Epistles of John," *The Interpreter's Bible.* Vol. 12. G. A. Buttrick, ed. New York: Abingdon, 1957.

Hunt, A. S. and Edgar, C. C. *Select Papyri.* Loeb Classical Library. Vol. 1. Cambridge, Mass.: Harvard U., 1952.

Law, Robert. *The Tests of Life, A Study of the First Epistle of John.* Edinburgh: T. & T. Clark, 1909.

Lenski, R. C. H. *The Interpretation of the Epistles of St. Peter, St. John, and St. Jude.* Columbus, O.: Wartburg, 1945.

Metzger, Bruce M. *The Text of the New Testament.* New York: Oxford U., 1964.

Plummer, A. *The Epistles of S. John. The Cambridge Greek Testament for Schools and Colleges.* J. J. S. Perowne, ed. Cambridge: Cambridge U., 1894.

Robertson, Archibald T. *Word Pictures in the New Testament.* Vol. 6. New York: Harper, 1933.

Ross, Alexander. *Commentary on the Epistles of James and John. The New International Commentary on the New Testament.* Ned B. Stonehouse, ed. Grand Rapids: Eerdmans, 1954.

Ryrie, Charles C. "I, II, and III John," *The Wycliffe Bible Commentary.* Charles F. Pfeiffer and Everett F. Harrison, eds. Chicago: Moody, 1962.

Smith, David. "The Epistles of John," *The Expositor's Greek Testament.* Vol. 5. W. Robertson Nicoll, ed. Grand Rapids: Eerdmans, n.d.

Stott, John R. W. *The Epistles of John. The Tyndale Bible Commentaries.* R. V. G. Tasker, ed. Grand Rapids: Eerdmans, 1964.

Vincent, Marvin R. *Word Studies in the New Testament.* Vol. 2. New York: Scribner, 1908.

Westcott, Brooke F. *The Epistles of St. John.* Grand Rapids: Eerdmans, 1950.

White, R. E. O. *Open Letter to Evangelicals.* Grand Rapids: Eerdmans, 1964.